ESP The sixth sense

Brian Ward

Macdonald Guidelines

© Macdonald Educational Ltd. 1977

First published 1977
Macdonald Educational Ltd.
Holywell House
Worship Street
London EC2A 2EN

ISBN 0 356 06020 9
Printed and bound by
Waterlow (Dunstable) Ltd.

Contents

Information
- **4** Introduction
- **9** The occult
- **12** Telepathy and clairvoyance
- **18** Mind over matter
- **22** Mind over body
- **26** Messages from beyond
- **31** Reincarnation
- **34** Out of mind and body
- **36** Travels out of time
- **42** Psychic prodigies
- **46** Psychic frauds
- **50** The psychic significance of dreams
- **54** Animal ESP
- **58** Parascience
- **64** Fringe medicine

Activities
- **70** Dowsing
- **74** Telepathy and clairvoyance
- **76** Psychokinesis
- **78** Getting the message
- **80** Who's kidding who?
- **82** Preserving pyramid
- **83** Sheep or goat?

Reference
- **84** Biographies
- **89** Associations etc.
- **90** Book list
- **91** Glossary
- **94** Index

Introduction

Do you think of yourself as exceptionally lucky? Do you find that amazing 'coincidences' seem to be quite common? Maybe you have premonitions? Or can you always find something which the rest of the family is scouring the house for?

These are just some of the more common expressions of psychic ability, or extra-sensory perception, usually abbreviated to ESP. 'Extra-sensory' means that this is a faculty, or set of faculties, by which we can perceive events without the use of our normal senses.

When we look at an apple on a table close to us, reflected light conveys an image through our eyes, and into the brain, where we actually 'see' the apple. This process of sight is well understood, and is very reliable; our eyes seldom let us down.

But if the apple is in another room, out of 'sight', or even in a room a hundred miles away, and we can sometimes still 'see' it in our mind's eye, then provided it is not an imaginary apple, we will have received the visual image directly on our brain without the use of our eyes or any other normal sense—it must be ESP!

This process of eyeless sight is called clairvoyance, but many other forms of ESP are recognized. If another person had been looking at the 'out of sight' apple, for example, we could be receiving a signal directly from that person's mind. This would be telepathy.

These are just two of the phenomena covered by the loose description; ESP. It is something of a misnomer, however, because it is difficult to separate *knowledge* of events without the use of normal senses from some degree of ability to *control* events without apparent physical means.

Psychokinesis

Psychokinesis (PK) is a term which has been coined to describe the apparent ability of some people to influence physical events with the power of their mind; causing dice to constantly score sixes, for instance. But if the mind can 'push' the dice in this

The paranormal covers an enormous range of inexplicable phenomena. Mind-to-mind contact, moving objects with the power of the mind, and knowledge of the future are all faculties which a skilled psychic can use. Some of the phenomena of the paranormal, like survival after death, have important religious significance.

way, ESP must presumably still be used to determine where the desired face of the dice is at any moment as it rolls. Otherwise, when would the psychokinetic 'nudge' be given? A problem of this sort would tax the guidance system of a guided missile, yet a few talented people seem to be able to demonstrate such powers.

The general term used to describe all these phenomena of ESP and inexplicable mental powers is 'paranormal', also often called psi, after a letter of the Greek alphabet.

But is it scientific?

Why are these amazing powers not fully accepted by science and the general public? Probably three quarters of the population accept that some form of ESP or paranormal power exists, although some people do not realize that talents they accept as being fairly commonplace, such as dowsing, may be paranormal in origin.

To be acceptable to science, a phenomenon must be repeatable, when studied by another scientist. An experiment must be capable of being described fully, then be repeated by other investigators who obtain similar results, before becoming a respectable 'scientific' fact. It must be admitted that so far, there is no phenomenon connected with the paranormal which has been proven to the satisfaction of science in general. The paranormal is a 'wild talent', in that it only manifests itself under a few, poorly understood conditions, and experiments designed to prove its existence rarely produce consistent results. Indeed, the results of most scientific studies are so marginally better than the results one would expect from pure chance that involved statistics are required to make it possible even to suggest the presence of some paranormal ability.

On the other hand, respected scientific

J. B. Rhine initiated a revolution in the study of psychic phenomena, by using the methods of orthodox science to study events which had formerly been conveniently ignored by most scientists. The results he obtained convinced many scientists that the paranormal was a valid subject for study, and not just another form of occultism.

disciplines such as modern particle physics are based on equally slim evidence, as are some of the schools of psychiatry and psychology, such as those founded by Jung and Freud. In these sciences, as with the paranormal, the best evidence is not truly scientific, but is anecdotal, or based on single chance observations of odd phenomena.

These isolated and unrepeatable incidents are the basis for most people's belief in ESP and the paranormal. We have all experienced coincidences so extreme that a moment's thought almost rules out any possibility of them being mere chance. And for most of us, these impossible coincidences crop up so often that we no longer find them exceptional. Consider the num-

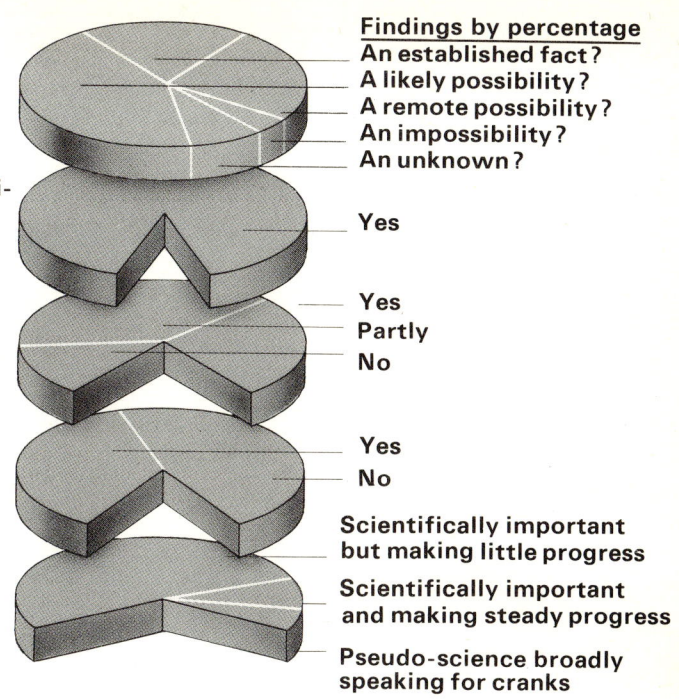

Questions	Findings by percentage
In your opinion is ESP	An established fact? A likely possibility? A remote possibility? An impossibility? An unknown?
Do you consider the investigation of ESP a legitimate scientific undertaking?	Yes
If so, does it fall within the province of academic psychology?	Yes Partly No
Are parapsychologists attacking the problem in the best way?	Yes No
Which statement most closely matches your attitude towards parapsychology?	Scientifically important but making little progress Scientifically important and making steady progress Pseudo-science broadly speaking for cranks

▲ The British magazine 'New Scientist' recently conducted a survey to determine the current attitude of its readers towards the paranormal.

ber of times someone has phoned you, a few minutes after you have been thinking of them or talking about them. These incidents don't prove a thing, scientifically, but they do demonstrate that the paranormal may have a place in our normal day-to-day lives. Proof of the paranormal in the laboratory may rest on abstruse experiments with no obvious practical application, but it is quite possible that the paranormal is merely a faculty or ability which we can only exercise imperfectly, if at all.

Is ESP a faculty we are slowly evolving; the next step in man's evolution, only this time on a purely mental level? Or is it an ancient talent now almost lost to us? If this is the case, should we not be studying the 'sixth sense' of animals?

Tomorrow's science?

Recent surveys show that scientists now regard the paranormal as a respectable subject for research, although a few die-hards fiercely resist *any* such work. Their attitude is understandable, for if the paranormal were once unequivocally proved, most scientific experiments would overnight become invalid. If psychokinesis works, then the experimenter could be unconsciously making the results of his experiment fit his own theories.

Unfortunately, the past history of the study of the paranormal does nothing to allay the fears of the sceptics, being dogged with fraud and sloppy experiments. However, the new science of parapsychology has now dawned, and perhaps the next few years may make the paranormal thoroughly respectable.

The occult

Two hundred years or so ago, the phenomena we now class as 'paranormal' were much more readily acceptable than they are today. But they were not thought to be the product of the mind; rather the result of trafficking with the Devil. Reading other people's minds, knowledge of the future, causing objects to move without touching them, and more particularly, talking with the dead, were all talents peculiar to witches, and were frequently punishable by death. We are not yet free from this attitude, which is responsible for the unease most people feel about the paranormal, and the respectful fear with which many treat those with paranormal powers.

Yet the phenomena have a long and respectable history. As far back as recorded history can be traced, priests and magicians have attempted to discover the future, by various forms of divination. These might involve casting coloured pebbles at random, and interpreting the patterns they made as they fell. In ancient Mesopotamia, animals were sacrificed to the gods, and their livers examined for significant patterns or bumps, rather as the 19th century phrenologists traced a person's character by measuring the bumps on his head. In other cultures, an enemy might be sacrificed, and his entrails examined for portents of the future.

John Dee

In the time of Elizabeth I, in the late 16th century, Dr John Dee undertook serious studies of the occult, and the results he obtained were remarkably similar to those of the psychical researchers of the early 20th century. Dee was a scholar, with a library containing more than 4,000 books —the largest in England at the time. He made the first English translation of the mathematical treatises of Euclid, and his scientific and philosophical works were influential and respected. His other, occult, studies were less respectable, however, and led to his persecution by the authorities and eventual financial ruin.

Dee rediscovered a whole system for speaking with spirits. With the help of a medium called Edward Kelly, Dee made contact with 'angels' who spoke to Kelly

◀ Tarot cards are variants of ordinary playing cards which bear heavily symbolic pictures, making them suitable for divination. This card depicts Mercury, from a set designed for the occultist Aleister Crowley.

▶ Shamans are priest magicians found in many primitive northern tribes. This Lapp shaman is prosphesying with the aid of a magic drum which he rests on his back.

▲ Dr John Dee was an Elizabethan magician, astrologer, and mathematician who fell into disrepute after being accused of attempting to raise the dead in order to force the corpse to prophesy.

through a crystal, or through a curved mirror of black glass. This is the technique of scrying, still widely used by clairvoyants today. Dee's angels did not impart any valuable information to him, but they did instruct him, through Kelly, in an unknown language called Enochian. Using Enochian, spirits could be summoned to do the magician's bidding. It is still used by some modern magicians, although the results they obtain are no more reliable than were those of Dr Dee.

Mesmer

Another early exponent of the art of the paranormal was Franz Anton Mesmer (1734-1815), the discoverer of 'animal magnetism', which led to the modern study of hypnotism. Mesmer believed that planets affected the health of people, through a process akin to magnetism, so he began treating the sick by means of magnets passed over their bodies. Soon he decided that this healing force came through him, rather than the magnets, and began healing by means of passes of his hands, or by objects 'charged' by being handled by him.

His increasing fame led him to go into 'mass production'. Mesmer had constructed a huge tub filled with water and iron filings, from which protruded a series of iron rods. Round the tub sat Mesmer's patients, each applying the end of one of the rods to the diseased part of their bodies. Mesmer moved among them clad in flowing robes, and made 'magnetic passes', which caused many of his patients to fall to the ground in a fit. He caused such a sensation that the French government set up an investigating commission, among whose members was Benjamin Franklin. This concluded that some of Mesmer's patients were cured, although his 'passes' were flagrantly immoral.

Mesmer's work soon fell into disrepute, but helped lay the foundation for the modern use of hypnotism in psychiatry. It has also been revived by the modern interest of parapsychologists in the use of hypnosis to heighten paranormal powers. His work eventually led to recognition of the power of suggestion on a susceptible mind. Many apparent paranormal phenomena have turned out to be illusory, although they are entirely convincing to those experiencing them. (The Indian Rope Trick is a case in point.)

The Fox sisters

From Mesmer's pseudo-scientific studies, investigation of the paranormal changed direction with the first stirrings of Spiritualism in 1848. In the small New York town of Hydesville, the Fox family had been worried for some time by strange and inexplicable rappings heard in the night. One night, however, one of the Fox children, Kate, invited the phantom rappings to copy the snapping of her fingers. To her surprise, they did, quite reliably, and Kate and her sister Margaret were soon able to use a simple code for asking questions of the spirit, which always tapped out its answer. The spirit claimed to be that of a murdered peddlar, who had been buried beneath the house, and oddly enough, 56 years later, a skeleton was found buried in the cellar wall.

The fame of the Fox sisters spread, and they began to give public demonstrations of spirit rapping. The fashion spread like wildfire through the western world, and mediums began to produce more dramatic phenomena. In 1888, Margaret Fox shocked the growing spiritualist movement by claiming that she had produced the rapping by cracking the joints of her toes. By then, however, the movement had gained too much momentum to be stopped.

Interest centred on the nature of the spirits communicating with the mediums. If, as appeared, they were not disembodied beings in their own right, but were actually the spirits of a person recently dead, then the ancient goal of survival after death would be finally proven, once and for all. The phenomena had important religious, scientific, and philosophical implications, and towards the end of the century, serious study began. These new physical mediums were now apparently able to cause bunches of flowers to materialize from the air; to cause trumpets and accordions to float about and to play; sometimes to produce the spirits themselves in visible form. The trouble was that these manifestations generally took place in almost total darkness, and so could not easily be studied.

The SPR

Formal study began with a number of scholars and scientists in Britain, at first working independently. In 1882, several of these workers agreed to form a society for the study of these inexplicable phenomena; the Society for Psychical Research. Among its objectives were to study: the effects of one mind on another; hypnotism and clairvoyance; extra-sensory perception; apparitions and the phenomena of the seances. With these objectives, the SPR initiated the modern study of the paranormal.

▶ In the 16th and 17th centuries, witches were accused of being able to produce, with the aid of the Devil, the phenomena which were later seen in seances. Floating in the air in the seance room or flying on a broomstick are not so very different, and both are forms of levitation.

Telepathy and clairvoyance

Telepathy and clairvoyance are the classical paranormal phenomena—in fact, they are the talents properly known as ESP. They are difficult to separate. Telepathy is usually regarded as being the paranormal transmission of information from one mind to another, while in clairvoyance, information is gained without the help of another mind. In some ways, telepathy can be thought of as a clairvoyant reading of another person's mind. In practice, it is difficult to set up telepathic experiments which exclude clairvoyance, although with a little ingenuity, telepathy itself can be excluded from experiments.

These talents of producing manifestations of ESP are delicate and tend to disappear in the cold and unsympathetic light of the laboratory. But some evidence of ESP can be detected in more normal surroundings. The close affinity of twins is legendary, and most people have known of twins who are simultaneously taken ill, even though they may be living many miles apart and have no knowledge of each other's illness.

There are very many well authenticated examples of individuals who have known of their twin's death by paranormal means, presumably as a result of a breaking of some imperceptible psychic link, or a telepathic sense of loss.

This close mental link between twins has been demonstrated in a unique series of experiments. Twins were wired up to an

▶ A perverse problem with telepathy experiments is that the message transmitted is often only symbolic of the target. In this trial, a girl is trying to send a mental picture of a church tower.

electroencephalograph machine, which measures the tiny currents flowing through the brain. When one twin relaxed so that his brain began to produce the electrical patterns typical of the resting mind, the machine attached to his twin in another room immediately recorded the same resting patterns. This experiment did not show the transmission of messages, but rather the telepathic nature of changes of mood.

Psychic bonds

But no close blood relationship is necessary to explain the similar phenomena often experienced between husband and wife, or between close friends. When both people begin to say the same thing simultaneously, or react apparently spontaneously to some minor event, this could be telepathy. It could also simply mean that they know each other so well that they react identically to any given event, however.

The bond between mothers and their newborn babies is less easy to explain away. Most mothers seem to have a strong telepathic bond, and know instinctively when their child is distressed. This would obviously be a talent of tremendous biological advantage, and if it actually happens, we would expect evolution to speedily build it into the genetic pattern of the entire human race. This telepathic bond certainly seems to exist, although like other paranormal phenomena, it is difficult to demonstrate, and disappears in later life. Perhaps once we learn to communicate in other ways, this unreliable faculty is discarded in favour of speech.

The Russians have carried out experi-

▶ The receiver records an impression of a wedding cake. Is it a 'hit' or a 'miss'? His response is recognizably the same shape as the target, although its size and function is wildly out.

ments in a submarine in which baby rabbits were killed at regular intervals, while many miles away, on land, the brain waves of the mother rabbit showed distinct changes at the moment each died.

Weighing the evidence

The chief difficulty in studying ESP is the transient and erratic nature of the phenomena. The reason for this refusal of ESP to appear to order is difficult to understand, but it does seem to be very much dependent on the subject's mood. Most successful exponents of ESP, as well as many mediums, perform best when they are in a relaxed and slightly dreamy state. The tense excitement of a successful experiment may temporarily enhance the subject's powers of ESP, but in the long term, the best results are obtained while the subject is fully relaxed. The electroencephalograph, or EEG, is often used to train subjects to produce the alpha rhythm, the brain waves characteristic of this mood. Many scientists feel that these 'altered states of consciousness' are of critical importance, and have studied the psychic abilities of yogis and people trained in transcendental meditation, Zen, and other contemplative techniques. So far, however, no reliable results have been obtained.

So does ESP really occur? Or is it just wishful thinking? The evidence, is compelling enough for Prof. Hans Eysenck, Professor of Psychology at London University to have commented:

'Unless there is a gigantic conspiracy involving some 30 University departments all over the world, and several hundred highly respected scientists in various fields, many originally hostile to the claims of the psychical researchers, the only conclusion the unbiased observer can come to must be that there does exist a small number of people who obtain knowledge existing either in other people's minds, or in the outer world, by means as yet unknown to science.' 20 years later, there are probably hundreds of laboratories, and thousands of researchers still trying to demonstrate the elusive ESP.

The Zener card experiment

Scientists began to sit up and take interest in ESP back in 1934, when J. B. Rhine, at Duke University in North Carolina began to publish the results of a series of tests he had carried out. In an attempt to overcome the unreliable results of early work, Rhine simplified the tests so that the results would

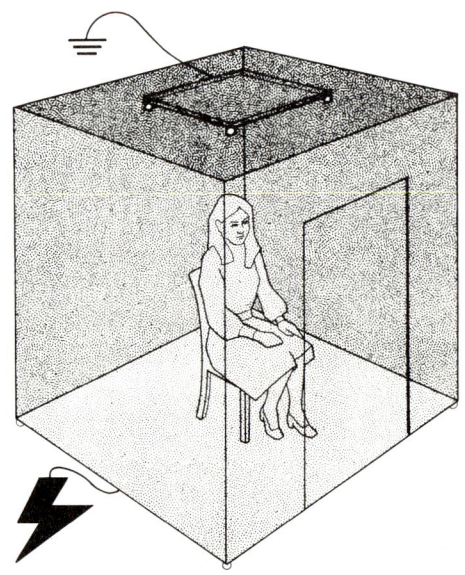

▶ The Faraday cage is a cube constructed of fine copper mesh, which is electrically charged, while the subject of the experiment sits on an insulated pad inside the cage. In theory, no radiation can pass into the cage, so if ESP occurs, it must work on some totally unexplained form of energy. In practice, the use of the cage seems to *enhance* ESP ability.

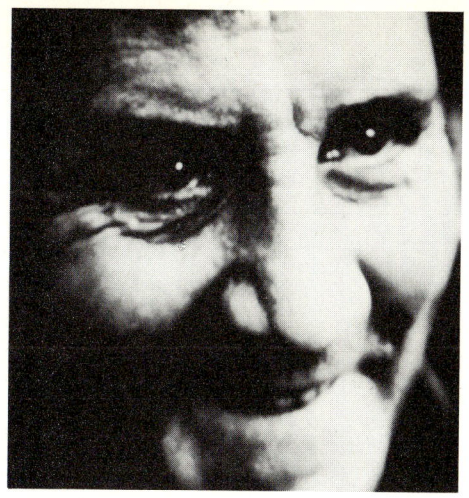

▲ Peter Hurkos is a Dutch psychic who is famous for his clairvoyant abilities. He has helped the police trace wanted criminals on many occasions, and has been responsible for the arrest and life imprisonment of a murderer.

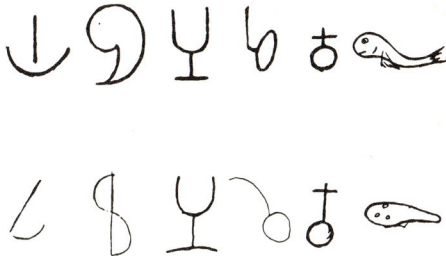

▼ In 1880, Malcolm Guthrie carried out a telepathy experiment with 'Miss E', with the results shown below. Guthrie drew the drawings in the top row, while 'Miss E' received the slightly distorted variants shown underneath. The similarities are enough to make chance very unlikely.

be completely unambiguous. His innovation was the deck of Zener cards, a pack of 25 cards, containing five of each of several simple symbols; cross, star, circle, square, and wavy lines. These were shuffled and turned over one at a time by a 'sender', while a 'receiver' tried to guess the cards as they were turned, and recorded his guess on a chart. For clairvoyance tests, the subject guessed the identity of cards placed face-down in front of the experimenter.

This very simple set-up produced some very significant results. When the cards are shuffled, and one is selected at random, there is a one in five chance of predicting which of the five symbols is being picked — by chance. If you go through the whole set, then by the mathematical laws of chance, you would expect to guess correctly five times. Quite often, by chance, you would be lucky enough to guess more accurately, and this would be quite unremarkable. But if you continue to score better than chance, the probability increases that some paranormal force is at work. If you make enough guesses, this conclusion can be overwhelming. Suppose you press on to make 10,000 guesses; by chance you would expect 2,000 correct guesses, but you actually make 2,200 correct guesses. Statistics tell us that the odds *against* this being pure chance are one in two million!

Rhine persevered with his tests for long enough to obtain compelling results. In one of the most noted experiments conducted under his supervision at Duke University, carried out by Dr Pratt with a subject called Woodruff in 1939, results of 1,700,000 to one against chance were obtained.

Towards a science

Rhine's results were immediately challenged by people who said that the statistical method of analyzing the trials was at fault; this was soon proved to be incorrect, however. Others claimed that the experimental conditions allowed cheating, and Rhine replied by tightening up the control on the experiments. Yet another suggestion was that the cards were not properly shuffled. This was an important point, for even with these huge odds Woodruff had only scored marginally better than chance would predict and only a few cards would need to escape shuffling to influence the results in this way. This problem was overcome by the use of mechanical shuffling, or tables of random numbers which determined the positions of the cards in the pack.

Tests held later showed up another important phenomenon which has since been found to apply to most subjects with ESP. The best subjects start off with fairly low scores, then as their confidence builds up, they begin to make better progress. But after the thousands of guesses each is subjected to, their abilities seem to deteriorate and eventually disappear completely. This process is usually spread over a number of years, but has meant that the most promising subjects are usually only available for study for a limited time.

How does ESP work?

The nature of ESP has completely eluded all researchers. Until fairly recently, it was confidently assumed that ESP was some sort of magnetic or electrical effect. A number of ingenious tests proved that this was not the case, however. Any electrical energy must become weaker with distance, but ESP has been shown to operate quite independently of distance. 'Senders' have been able to transmit pictures and ideas across the Atlantic to recipients thousands of miles away, and the astronaut Ed Mitchell managed to send back telepathic messages from orbit around the moon—in a private experiment *not* sponsored by NASA.

The use of a Faraday cage was even more conclusive. This wire box, charged with electricity, should have prevented almost all forms of radiation from reaching the subject inside. Instead, with all outside electrical 'noise' blanketed by the cage, the subjects' performances were notably enhanced.

Current theories revolve about the possibility of sub-atomic particles being responsible for ESP. These almost imperceptible pieces of energy are among the few forms of energy capable of penetrating the Faraday cage, although how they could be detected or used by the brain is a complete mystery.

Different types of experiments have provided further clues to the nature of ESP. In some of these the subject tries to guess a word or picture being studied by the 'sender', and it is notable that their responses often symbolize the 'target', rather than describe it accurately. For example, a drawing of a boat with a triangular sail might be interpreted as a pyramid, or as an ocean liner. It is as though the information is passed through to the brain as a coded message, which the brain translates into what it sees as the nearest appropriate symbol. Perhaps rather than passing on the message like a telephone, ESP simply activates an appropriate memory already present in the brain, but which may not exactly represent the target.

▶ In any ESP trial the experimenter and the subject can easily bias the results quite inadvertently. To avoid these errors, and to eliminate accusations of fraudulent tests, modern parapsychologists use automated equipment wherever possible. This German ESP test machine selects targets automatically, and records the subject's response on a computer.

▼ **Zener card tests**
1 A typical target sequence in an ESP trial, using the standard type of Zener cards. A one in five chance of successful guessing is expected. **2** When the subject has made four hits, the results are exactly those expected by pure chance. **3** When the subject makes eight hits, it is possible that ESP is operating. **4** Sometimes the subject guesses the card *before* the target; the displacement effect which often complicates the results of trials.

Mind over matter

Psychokinesis or PK is the technical term which describes the eerie ability of a very few talented people to move objects with the power of their minds, sometimes quite inadvertently.

The objects moved vary from ordinary small objects like cigarettes and coins to more ephemeral substances like smoke. In some cases, individual molecules within an object appear to be moved. This would be one explanation for the much-publicized spoon-bending of the Israeli psychic, Uri Geller. Rearrangement of the molecules could cause the metal to bend and ultimately, to break.

There are more severe barriers to the acceptance of PK than there are to telepathy. As our nervous system operates on minute pulses of electricity, it is not too difficult to imagine that we might have some as yet unknown method of picking up these tiny signals in another person's brain. This would involve only a small leap forward in our present knowledge. But there is no such convenient theory available to explain PK. The objects moved are frequently not even

▲ Hand-thrown dice do not always fall at random, so for PK experiments in which subjects try to score particular numbers, an automatic dice-rolling machine is used.

◄ In types of seances common around the turn of the century, mediums were restrained to try and stop them using their hands and feet, while tables and chairs floated in the air.

magnetic, so the way in which they are moved is a complete mystery.

Dicing with PK

As with ESP, J. B. Rhine made a detailed scientific study of PK. Just as he had tried to simplify the phenomena he was studying by the use of Zener cards, so he began his studies on PK by trying to find people who could affect the fall of dice. This idea resulted from a casual remark made by a gambler, '... who said that upon occasion when he was properly keyed up, he could make the dice fall as he willed'.

Once more, the results obtained were much better than would be expected by chance alone. Rhine improved his experiments by using a mechanical dice-shaker, to avoid any possibility of his subject cheating and influencing the fall of the dice by 'normal' means.

Two serious criticisms of this work remained, however. The first is that dice do *not* fall entirely at random. Because the spots are bored out on each face, the 'six' is the lightest side, and tends to come up more frequently than the others, thus biasing the results. The other problem is of much more practical value. Casinos throughout the world operate by taking a small percentage of the cash passing across their tables. If anyone really could affect the fall of the dice or spin of the roulette wheel consistently, the casinos would very soon be out of business—or else would refuse to deal with such a consistently 'lucky' gambler.

The obvious solution to such criticisms was to concentrate the experiments on simpler problems. Helmut Schmidt, Rhine's successor at Duke University, produced an elegant experiment which demolished these criticisms, and has led to a grudging acceptance of PK as a scientifically suitable subject for study.

Schmidt concentrates his efforts on persuading his subjects to try moving the simplest object of all—the electron. In the Schmidt machine, described more fully on page 62, the random appearance of an electron causes one of a series of bulbs arranged in a circle to light at random. The subject's task is to force them to light in turn; many have succeeded, and the critics have not yet produced a plausible explanation.

The amazing Mikhailova

Not all laboratory experiments are carried out with such exotic equipment, however, as a few very powerful psychics seem to be

◀ At a public demonstration in the Conway Hall in London, the medium Colin Evans floated in the air at a height of five metres, for a total of one minute. This was a rare and inexplicable demonstration of levitation.

Nelya Mikhailova seems to have overcome the usual problem of the psychic, whose powers generally refuse to display themselves upon request. Many earlier studies of PK, or even of levitation of the whole body, had been of those highly unsatisfactory demonstrations which took place in almost total darkness, in the seance rooms.

The poltergeist

A common and dramatic example of PK working in an uncontrolled manner is the phenomenon of poltergeists (literally 'noisy spirits' in German). In a home afflicted by a poltergeist, strange rapping noises are heard, objects disappear or are moved about inexplicably, and worst of all, things are hurled violently about, causing considerable damage. Lumps of coal, bottles, cups and saucers may all fly across the room, and sometimes even heavy wardrobes are moved. Oddly enough, the occupants are very seldom injured, even though they feel the poltergeist is actually attacking them. Usually they leave the house in terror, and the phenomena then apparently cease.

In spite of the currently fashionable practice of exorcizing such 'haunted' houses, malicious spirits need not be assumed to be the cause. In practically every authenticated case of poltergeist activity, an adolescent or child has been present in the house, or associated closely with the house. And frequently, the child has been shown to be under some sort of stress at the time the incidents occur. For this reason, poltergeists are generally thought to be an example of very powerful PK abilities which are being unconsciously used by the child.

Significantly, the poltergeist activity fades as the child becomes mature and usually disappears by late adolescence.

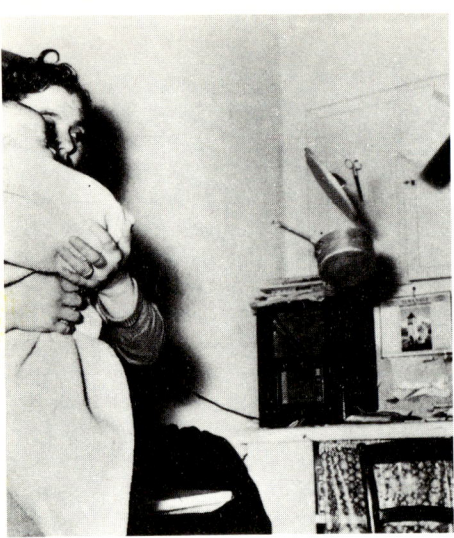

▲ Poltergeists are responsible for throwing various items around in an afflicted house. They are generally thought to be a form of PK which operates erratically and inadvertently.

able to produce much more easily demonstrated phenomena. Many of these psychics have been found behind the Iron Curtain, and of them, Nelya Mikhailova (also known as Nelya Kulagina) has consistently produced the most extraordinary results.

Nelya Mikhailova, a Leningrad housewife, has for a number of years been studied intensively by Russian scientists, undergoing literally hundreds of tests. She is able to cause a compass needle to rotate without touching it, and apparently at will has made small objects move about the surface of a table. On one occasion, she even made a small piece of bread slide across the table, and jump into her mouth. She was also able to cause smoke floating in a closed container to drift into separate layers, and most astonishing of all, to separate the yolk of an egg from its white, then to recombine them.

Through small electrodes attached to the scalp, scientists were able to measure the electrical signals produced by the brain during PK.

Heart rate was measured throughout the experiment and showed that the heart beat became very fast and irregular.

Other body functions were continuously measured, and showed that the subject was undergoing a high level of stress.

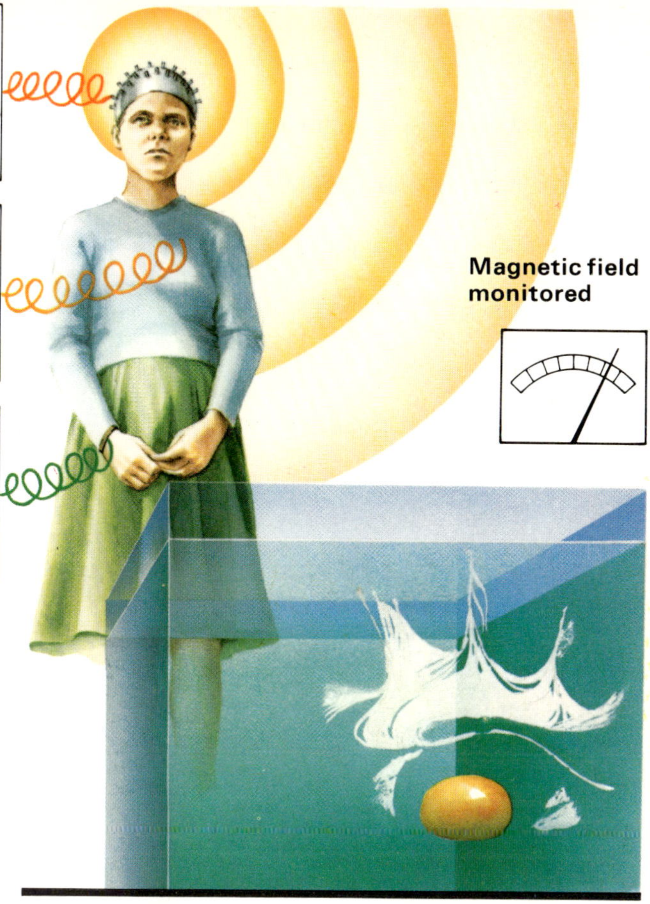

Magnetic field monitored

During one experiment, the Soviet psychic Nelya Mikhailova separated the yolk of an egg from its white, and then replaced it. She has been extensively studied in the laboratory, and provides an insight into the body changes that occur during PK. The electrical activity within her brain rises to very high levels, and at the same time, her pulse rate increases to 240 per minute. The magnetic field around her body also increases in intensity, and when all this activity reaches a peak, these functions become synchronized, fluctuating together in rhythm. At this point PK is produced and she is able to move objects about without touching them. After all this intense activity, Nelya loses as much as 1 kg in weight.

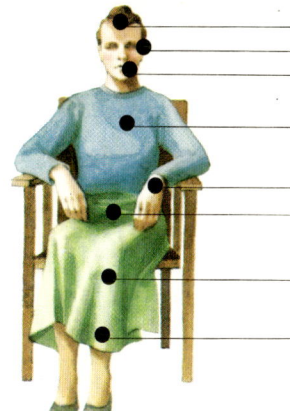

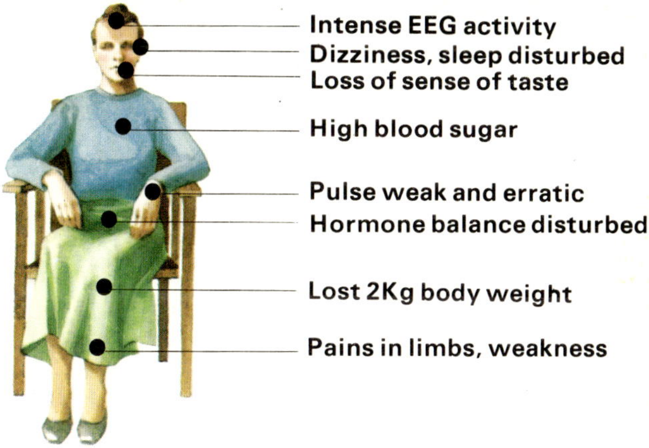

- **Intense EEG activity**
- **Dizziness, sleep disturbed**
- **Loss of sense of taste**

- **High blood sugar**

- **Pulse weak and erratic**
- **Hormone balance disturbed**

- **Lost 2Kg body weight**

- **Pains in limbs, weakness**

Mind over body

Our minds have an almost infinite capacity for self-deception, and for the deception of other minds. This trickery can encompass mood, what we see and hear, and even affect the functions of the body.

We know that the functioning of our brain is physical rather than spiritual in nature. Complex chemical reactions within our brain cells power the brain itself, producing myriads of flickering electrical discharges which collectively make up the process of thought. Although the workings of the brain are fairly well understood, the effects it has on our behaviour are certainly not. Some of these effects are so bizarre and inexplicable that they may be conveniently regarded as paranormal.

The legendary Indian Rope Trick illustrates this facility for self deception. The Chief of Police in Calcutta and a subordinate once witnessed and photographed the famous event. They watched the rope thrown into the air, and witnessed the fakir follow his assistant up the rope, where both vanished. The fakir soon climbed back down the rope, with a blood-stained sword. These amazing events were not, of course, supported by the pictures on the developed film.

A similar incident was photographed in the grounds of an official residency in India in 1934. These pictures show the rope lying on the ground, and the small boy creeping off to hide in the bushes. This in spite of the fact that many other witnesses believed they had seen the famed Rope Trick performed (although in 1875 the Viceroy had offered £10,000 to anyone who could demonstrate it, and had no takers). In these instances, by mass hallucination, hypnosis, or some form of hysteria, the fakirs had

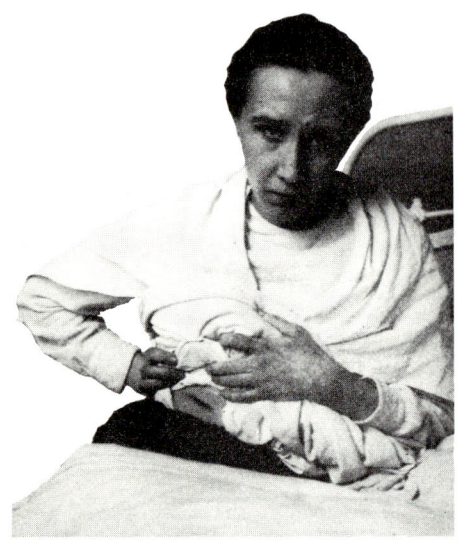

▲ Teresa Neumann was a visionary who bore stigmata, or spontaneous wounds corresponding to the wounds of Christ. These wounds never healed, and bled regularly on the Thursday of each week.

somehow managed to superimpose their own versions of reality on the onlookers, and in doing so were influencing the physical events going on inside their brain cells.

Biofeedback

We can of course do this ourselves, to our own minds. We can daydream, or work ourselves up into all sorts of emotions. We can also exert unprecedented influence over the parts of our bodies we usually consider to be beyond normal control. There is no acceptable medical explanation for the ability of many eastern mystics to be able to slow their pulse rate down to imperceptible levels, or to reduce their rate of breathing to one or two inhalations each minute.

Although we apparently should not be able to do so, with the proper training, any of us can vary the rate at which our hearts beat, alter our blood pressure, and even raise and lower the temperature of the skin on selected parts of the body. This is accomplished by the techniques of biofeedback. If we are not aware of the functioning of parts of our bodies, we are generally not able to consciously affect them. But if, using a biofeedback machine, we can sense our pulse rate, monitor blood pressure, or measure the temperature of our skin, then we can learn to vary them at will.

Using the same techniques, we can also learn to produce the states of mind in which ESP is believed to manifest itself, such as the production of alpha waves; the brain waves characteristic of relaxed thought.

Such self-control, either physical or mental, can be used for medical purposes. Techniques of relaxation are used to treat a number of illnesses, either by mystical techniques or by biofeedback.

Control of pain is one technique which ranges from a useful ability to reduce irritating pain, through anaesthesia during surgical operations, to the spectacular eastern rituals which involve slashing the participants with swords, or piercing the flesh with long needles.

Stigmata

The mind can prevent pain; it can also produce pain, and actual physical injury. For hundreds of years it has been known that certain Christian mystics and saints produced stigmata. These are wounds or marks appearing on the skin, which are said to represent the wounds on Christ's body—

▲ The power of the mind over the body is such that while lying on a bed of nails, Rodinos Kotsoudis has a block of granite smashed on his chest with a sledgehammer, without causing him any injury.

◄ Under hypnosis, a normal person can have unprecedented physical strength. Normally it would be quite impossible for this girl to support the weight of a full-grown man on her outstretched body, resting only on heels and neck.

nail-marks on the hands and feet, scars from the crown of thorns on the forehead, and the spearmark in the side.

These stigmata generally appear only on the most devout, after long periods of meditation and ecstatic prayer. In medieval times they were considered to be signs of great holiness, but in the more sceptical 19th century were generally put down to outright fraud. More recently, however, study has shown that many stigmata are genuine, and are not simple self-inflicted wounds. In a few cases, stigmatics were seen to open their wounds quite unconsciously, and this has been attributed to a form of hysteria. But when Louise Lateau, one of the most famous stigmatics, was studied in the late 19th century, her arm was enclosed in a glass apparatus, and blood still welled up though her *unbroken* skin. The actual stigmata vary widely between different people. In some cases there are simply inflamed or pigmented marks on the skin. Others have actual wounds, which sometimes remain open because of continuous deep-seated infection. In the most remarkable types, like Louise Lateau, blood simply oozes through the skin, or large blisters appear on days of particular religious significance.

Hypnotism and stigmata

The self-willed nature of stigmata is emphasized by hypnotism. On Good Friday, 1932, 'Elizabeth', an Austrian child, was deeply impressed by seeing a film of the suffering of Christ, and developed severe pains in her hands and feet. The hypnotist Dr Lechler gave her the hypnotic suggestion that overnight, wounds would develop at the site of the pains. They did, and he was also able to persuade her to produce tears of blood and the marks of the crown of thorns. He was able to film the marks before causing them to heal, also by hypnotic suggestion.

Exactly the same effects have been produced in hypnotized people, without the spiritual interpretation of stigmata. The best known of these was a 'shell-shocked' sailor studied in 1917. He was hypnotized, and told that he was about to be touched with a red-hot poker. In fact, his arm was touched by the hypnotist's finger, and within a few hours, a large watery blister had formed.

How can hypnotism, or self-hypnosis, have these dramatic effects on the body and mind? The reason for its effects on the body is quite unknown. The effects of hypnotism on the mind and on paranormal abilities are still fiercely debated.

There is no clear understanding or agreement as to what the hypnotized state really is. The popular picture of a hypnotized person in an almost insensible state is quite inadequate, for studies of brain waves show that the hypnotized subject is fully conscious, although highly responsive to suggestion.

Its main relevance to the study of the

◀ At a religious parade in Singapore, a Chinese medium in a state of trance supports large banners which are spiked through his shoulder muscles, but cause no bleeding, and do not appear to cause any pain.

▼ At a Hong Kong festival, firewalkers step through a blaze without burning themselves. There is still argument as to how this is done without causing blistering. There is certainly no trickery involved, as many casual observers have been led through the fire without being injured.

paranormal is that it allows the subject to quickly enter the state of consciousness most suitable for the production of the phenomena being studied. This may be telepathy or PK. It is very often mediumship, for most mediums are found to enter a self-induced hypnotic trance while working. This is both an aid to concentration, which excludes all outside distractions, and at the same time a method of inducing a state of dissociation; a relaxed mood where reality itself becomes unreal, and the faint images running through the less accessible corners of the mind come to the surface.

Hypnosis has become a powerful tool for the parapsychologist. With its aid, promising subjects can be trained to strengthen their abilities, and in some cases, promising improvements in their scores during ESP tests have been noted.

Messages from beyond

One major part of the study of the paranormal is the question of life after death. Do we survive death in any recognizable form, and if so, can the dead contact the living?

This searching problem was the main reason for the formation of the Society for Psychical Research, and for many similar organizations in other countries. The search for evidence of survival takes many forms. It varies from the scholarly study of the work of expert mediums, to a form of religion. Spiritualist churches have a wide popular following in most European countries, and in Brazil, the Spiritists as they are known, form by far the largest of the country's many religious groups.

All such groups base their popular appeal on one premise; the possibility of contacting a loved one who has recently died. In addition, the spirit of the deceased is expected to have access to a wide body of knowledge not normally accessible to the living. Consequently, many people look to the spirits for guidance as to their day-to-day lives. Most people attending services or seances, however, are seeking spiritual solace, and find the experience both satisfying and rewarding. Almost all groups attempting to contact the spirit world do so with the aid of a medium; a person who can readily enter a trance state, in which it is possible to contact the spirits.

The techniques they use are varied, but most mediums fall quickly into a state of light trance before they begin to communicate. The professional medium usually begins by giving her clients, or sitters as they are known, a few basic background facts—usually the type of information one would expect to be known only by the sitter. The sitter is expected to participate

Rosemary Brown is an English medium who has written a vast amount of music which she believes has been dictated to her by long-dead composers. Modern experts are mixed in their opinions of the music she produces, some of which is too difficult for her to play herself. Some consider it to be unquestionably that of particular composers, such as Beethoven, Liszt, and many others. Other critics believe that it is simply a compilation of musical phrases found in the works of these composers. Yet another explanation is that it might be produced from Mrs Brown's subconscious mind, although this does not mean that she would be aware that it came from within her.

by confirming the statements made by the medium, and helping the medium to build on the information already given. This information is generally amplified by additional advice given to the medium by a spirit, whom he or she usually attempts to get the sitter to identify.

This type of mediumship sometimes produces quite remarkable results, with facts being revealed which astonish or sometimes embarrass the sitter. However, most of the information imparted is already present in the mind of the sitter, and so we cannot exclude telepathy as an alternative explanation to that of spirit communication.

Other forms of communication are less susceptible to this explanation. When a group of people take part in a seance, which may also include a medium, they usually use a mechanical device to help the spirits communicate; the ouija or the planchette. These are the latter-day versions of the table rapping or table tipping practiced by the early students of spiritualism.

The ouija and the planchette

The ouija is a simple device, often improvised by students of the occult. It consists of a smooth board, or up-turned mirror, around which are ranged the letters of the alphabet, and the words 'yes' and 'no'. The sitters rest their hands lightly on a pointer or glass, which slides about the board in response to questions, spelling out answers a letter at a time.

The planchette operates on a different principle, producing actual writing by means of a pencil attached to the freely moving board. This is a version of automatic writing, which may be carried out by one person or by a group. In those with highly developed powers of mediumship, automatic writing can be produced simply by holding a pen loosely over writing paper. When the medium is in a suitably relaxed state of mind, the pen begins to write, often without the medium being aware of its movements.

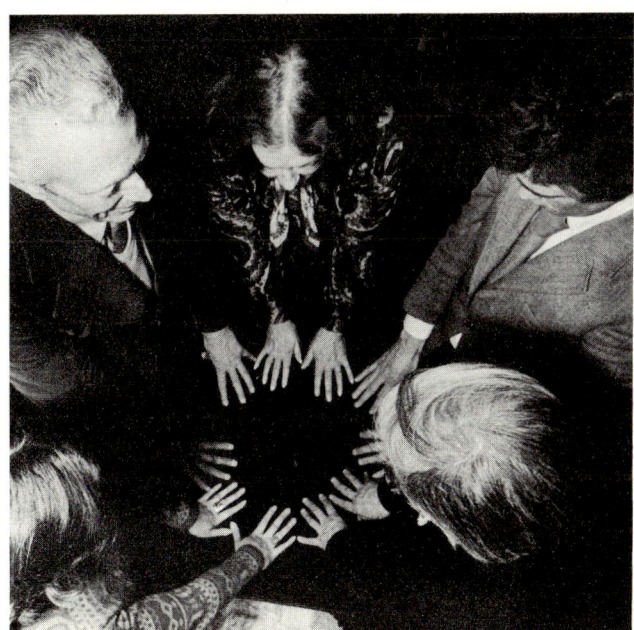

◀ A modern seance is conducted in the same way as those of the heyday of Spiritualism, nearly 100 years ago. The sitters and a medium are grouped about a table, often in subdued lighting, while the medium goes into a trance and attempts to contact the spirits. She may simply pass on information imparted to her by the spirits, or may speak in the recognizable voice of a dead person.

Using this technique, mediums have been able to produce some astonishing evidence of life after death, writing in the style, and with the same handwriting, as people long-dead. In some cases, mediums have produced long and accurate passages written in languages with which they were not at all familiar.

There are some 'normal' explanations for such feats, however, as it can often be shown that at some time in the medium's life, they had some contact with a person who spoke this particular language. Apparently it is possible to remember subconsciously with incredible accuracy, and in the trance state of mediumship such lost information comes to the surface of the mind through the intermediary of automatic writing. Automatic art, too has a place in the phenomena produced by mediums and in this field Mathew Manning is possibly the most accomplished psychic. Some examples of his automatic drawings are shown on page 44.

The spirit guides

Like many other paranormal phenomena, survival after death is not a subject which responds kindly to scientific investigation. In less formal surroundings, some mediums have been able to produce very convincing results, but in other cases, the subconscious workings of the mediums' minds become obvious.

This is very apparent in the names and identities of the spirit guides or 'controls', who serve as the medium's first contact

▶ Sir John Franklin was an explorer who vanished on an expedition near the North Pole, in 1847. When the Dutch psychic Gerard Croiset was handed one of Franklin's letters, sealed in an opaque envelope, he correctly stated that it had been written by a naval officer, the captain of a ship, which had broken up and sunk in the Atlantic in 1866 or 1868 — almost exactly correct except for the date.

The odds against making this sort of statement by pure guesswork are unthinkable. He could not have seen the contents of the letter. Even if he had been able to read it, the letter itself was quite inconsequential. This is one of the most convincing of all demonstrations of psychometry.

with the spirit world, and who continue to play a key part in their dealings with the spirits. These guides are usually Chinese philosophers, famous personalities of the past, or most popular of all, Red Indians. Most of these guides are quite obviously spurious characters, however well-intentioned the medium may be, and it may well be that the medium needs to rationalize the strange information she receives from her sitters by clairvoyance or telepathy, in order to provide an orderly framework for communicating to her client.

Yet with these reservations, some cases are very difficult to explain away. The classic example is the famous 'Cross Correspondences' case, which began soon after the death of the psychic researcher and

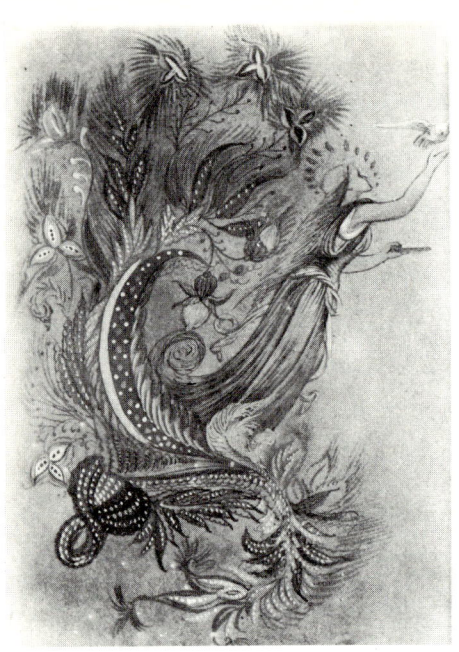

▲ In the late 19th century, Mrs Alaric Watts found that she could produce complex automatic paintings, in which her hand moved without her conscious control.

scholar F. W. H. Myers in 1901. Mediums began to receive messages, apparently from Myers, many of these in Greek and Latin. Over 30 years, thousands of pages of automatic writing were received, many containing extremely complex and abstruse literary allusions, which could only be deciphered by a scholar of similar ability to Myers himself. The writings cross-referred to messages being received by other mediums, often those with no direct contact with each other, except through the offices of the Society for Psychical Research. It is certainly difficult to imagine a fraud on such a scale as to involve dozens of mediums and scholars, and to be continued over such a long period as 30 years.

Even so, in 1962, Prof. Broad, an eminent former President of the Society for Psychical Research still wrote: 'I should be slightly more annoyed than surprised if I should find myself in some sense persisting immediately after the death of my present body. One can only wait and see, or alternatively (which is no less likely) wait and not see.'

◀ The 19th century medium Mlle Smith produced handwriting while in a trance, which was totally different from her usual style. This is an example of her normal writing.

◀ While in a trance, under the guidance of her 'control', 'Leopold', Mlle Smith produced this different form of script.

Reincarnation

One of the world's most widespread and persistent beliefs is that, under some circumstances, the personality of a dead person can become reborn in the living. Once reborn, they are seldom aware of their previous life, or lives, for many are re-incarnated time and time again.

There are elements of this belief in most of the world's major religions; Hindu, Buddhist, Sikh, Confucian, Muslim, Jewish, and Christian, and it also forms an important part in most occultist traditions.

There are no 'scientific' explanations for reincarnation; if it occurs, it is a mystical and spiritual phenomenon, which has significant religious implications. For most people experiencing the sensation of having lived a former life, the first intimations are of feelings of having been in an unfamiliar place once before, or of having once known

▲ In the famous Bridey Murphy case in the 1950s, an American housewife called Virginia Tighe recounted under hypnosis details of a previous life in a village in Ireland, which she had never visited herself. The details she gave were compelling, but none of the names or incidents could be verified, and it was subsequently found that she had been drawing on subconscious memories of Irish neighbours. This is a still from a film of her life.

Arthur Guirdham has found a group of people living in the southwest of England, including himself, who remember details of a previous existence as members of the medieval religious sect called Cathars. The Cathars were persecuted and eventually wiped out by the Inquisition in southern France, and detailed records of their trials and execution still survive in Church records. Many of the names and incidents recounted by the Guirdham group have been confirmed by study of these records, many of which have never before been published.

a person who is a total stranger. Modern researchers use hypnosis to help such sensitive individuals recall their former lives.

An American psychiatrist, Ian Stevenson, studied 20 possible cases of reincarnation, and one of these, involving a child living in a Lebanese village, provided extremely plausible evidence for reincarnation.

The boy, Imad Elawar, claimed to know a number of people unknown in his own village. One day he ran up to a perfect stranger, visiting from a neighbouring village, and claimed that he used to know him. Unusually in a case of this sort, Stevenson was able to interview the child *before* he had a chance to visit the scene of his former 'life', so when he eventually visited the village with the boy, he was able to verify the boy's story at first hand.

It appeared that Imad had been called Ibrahim Bouhamzy, and correctly described the house in which Ibrahim had lived, and many of the domestic fittings of his house.

Another odd case was a British girl who in 1931 began to speak in a strange language while in a trance. She appeared to have been an Egyptian temple dancer in a former life, and her communications in ancient Egyptian, which at the time was not well understood, were so impressive that an eminent Egyptologist was convinced of their authenticity.

Arnall Bloxham

Another modern researcher, Arnall Bloxham, has created something of a sensation with the well-authenticated examples of reincarnation he has discovered. Using hypnosis, he has helped his subjects to recall detailed accounts of their former lives.

One was a former sailor serving on a British frigate blockading the French coast during the Napoleonic wars. He died after

▶ Using hypnosis, Arnall Bloxham has been able to record the experiences of his subjects in former lives. Some of their information has been confirmed by historical experts, and has defied 'normal' explanation.

▼ An artist's impression of survival after death was given in Stanley Spencer's 'The Resurrection', showing the dead leaving their graves, in the churchyard of the small town of Cookham in southern England. Most of the people depicted are actual inhabitants of the town, and the artist showed himself twice in the picture, lying on a grave at the right, and leaning against a tomb near the church porch.

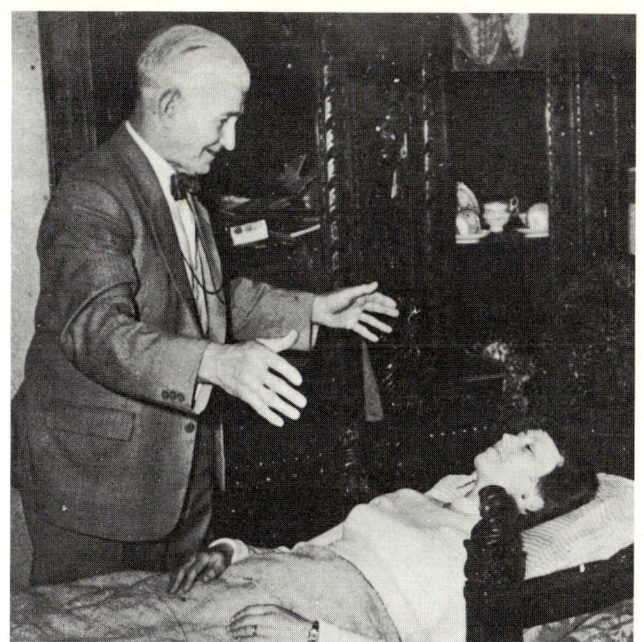

having his leg shot off—vividly described with harrowing screams on the tape recording of his account. Some of the details of life at sea in a Navy ship were completely new to Naval historians, but were subsequently verified by the Greenwich Maritime Museum.

Another of Bloxham's subjects believed herself to have been killed during a medieval pogrom against the Jews living in the ancient city of York. She describes the scene as Jews hidden in the crypt of a church were dragged out and slaughtered brutally.

This account did not arouse much interest as it was known that none of the churches in York had crypts. But quite recently, during renovation of one church, a hitherto unsuspected crypt was found beneath a floor, with its entrance bricked up. Once opened it was found to match the description given by Bloxham's subject in every detail.

Out of mind and body

Survival after death means that the mind can exist independently of the body, and that it is in some ways an independent entity. This raises the intriguing possibility that the mind might be able to become separated from the body *before* death, and to return to the body without harmful effects.

These 'out of the body' experiences are quite widespread, and have been closely studied in recent years. It has been found in one survey that 34 per cent of undergraduates interviewed at Oxford University and at some time had the experience of looking at themselves from outside their own bodies. Ernest Hemingway, Arthur Koestler, Virginia Woolf, D. H. Lawrence and a host of other respected writers have reported the same experience.

Out of the body experiences, or OOBEs, seem to occur spontaneously mostly under conditions of enormous physical stress, when life is actually threatened, or appears to be threatened. There are many accounts of people who have suffered heart attacks, or who are undergoing critical surgical operations, seeing doctors and nurses working furiously to resuscitate a body. They are able to observe this activity quite dispassionately, and it is often quite a long time before they realize that the 'body' is their own. They are usually able to make a distinct effort to return to their body, and once they have re-entered it they make a rapid return to consciousness.

The experience seems to be enjoyable; most people feel reluctant to make the effort to return, and some find they can drift off to see friends or relatives before being pulled back inexorably by returning consciousness.

In a typical case a drowning victim wrote: 'I watched my father at work on his boat, my brothers deadly frightened hanging to my spindly heels and I, my hair like seaweed pulled flat against the bottom of the float. Thus, while I drowned I saw my father turn and act; I saw my frightened

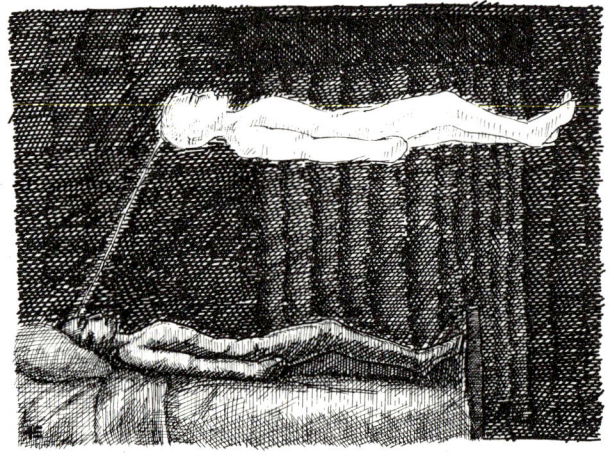

▶ Someone having an OOBE experience will find himself separated from his physical body. Sometimes the subject is able to travel at will, leaving his physical body behind for a while. This is very similar to the occultists' concept of an astral body which is normally confined within the physical body. According to this doctrine, the astral body can, with suitable training, leave the physical body and move freely, though attached to it by a cord.

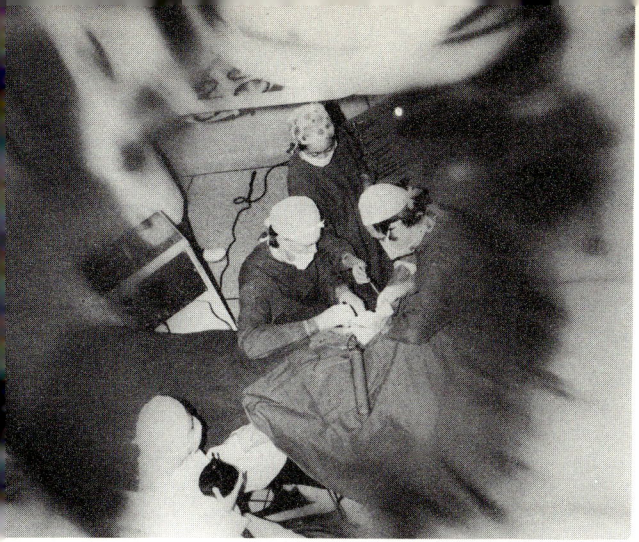

◀ People who have severe heart attacks, or who have nearly died on the operating table, quite often have the frightening experience of seeing themselves from the outside. They are not usually aware that anything is wrong until they recognize their own body, with doctors and nurses working over it. There is no sensation of pain or panic during such an out-of-the-body experience, and people are usually quite reluctant to force themselves to return to their physical bodies.

brothers run homewards; I saw the efforts to bring me back to life and *I tried not to come back.*'

Depersonalization

While undergoing an OOBE, many people have commented on the strange time distortions they experience. Everything goes on at a tranquil, dream-like pace, and the whole episode does often resemble a dream very closely.

The whole experience is very like a psychological condition known as depersonalization, in which one feels an air of unreality about the surroundings, and may also have hallucinations. This condition is quite common in people who are severely ill, or are suffering from drugs, and has also been found to affect most people suffering violent accidents. It is the cause of the familiar situation of 'seeing your life pass before you' at the moment an accident seems imminent, and it has been estimated that as many as half of all people involved in life-threatening accidents have some form of OOBE, seeing themselves from a distance.

So is the OOBE a genuine paranormal event, or simply a delusion of a mind under stress? The obvious proof would be to gain information not accessible by normal means, while in the OOBE condition. In a few cases, a different type of proof has been offered. When a person is on the point of death, they sometimes actually appear as an apparition before a close relative. These apparitions have sometimes been seen when the person involved is thousands of miles away, and generally look so realistic that the person seeing them is not at first aware of their true nature. The vision is usually authenticated by later hearing that the person seen had actually died at the time of the incident.

Such anecdotal accounts do not prove the existence of the OOBE, although they are otherwise difficult to explain except by telepathy or clairvoyance on the part of the person seeing the apparition.

Astral travel?

With long practice, some people are able to induce OOBE's more or less at will, so it is easy to set up quite simple experiments in order to determine whether they are actu-

▲ The ancient Egyptians believed that the soul or *ba* was a bird-faced being which hovered about the body after death, in a manner rather like that reported for OOBEs.

▲ This picture, 'L'amour des âmes', symbolizes for many people the freeing of the spirit from the body. It closely resembles some examples of automatic art.

ally able to obtain information while in this trance state. One parapsychologist, Charles Tart, experimented with a young woman who claimed that she sometimes found herself floating above her bed near the ceiling, looking down at her body. In the parapsychology laboratory, she was wired into an EEG machine, which recorded her brain waves, and asked to try to identify a five-figure number written on a card placed on a shelf seven feet above her bed. For each of the four nights of the experiment, she reported OOBEs, but only on the final night did she obtain the correct number, 25132.

She was not being observed continuously, so fraud cannot be entirely ruled out, although with the many fine wire leads of the EEG machine attached to her scalp, it is difficult to see how she could have climbed or reached up to the shelf without disturbing them. Although only one guess was made at the number, the success she achieved means that the results are statistically highly significant.

In another type of test, the experimenters have tried to exclude clairvoyance as a possible explanation for OOBE phenomena. In this ingenious test, the target is a letter 'd' on a screen inside a box. It can only be viewed through a hole in the box, behind which a mirror reverses the letter so that a 'b' is seen. The subject is instructed to go, in the form of an OOBE, into the other room, and report on the target. If he actually has an OOBE, and literally 'looks' through the hole at the target, he would report seeing the letter 'b'. If, on the other hand, he uses clairvoyance, the box will provide no more impediment than did the wall of the room, and he will see 'd'.

A variant on OOBE phenomena is the state of mind technically called 'transpersonal consciousness', in which a person feels themself fuse, both physically and mentally, with another. This appears to be a more spiritual experience than the relatively calm and detached emotions reported by those experiencing the usual type of OOBE.

Travels out of time

To discover the secrets of the future is man's oldest dream. The arts of prophecy, divination, and astrology all attempt to reveal the future, and their enormous and enduring appeal lies in the possibility of conducting one's life in such a way that knowledge of the future makes it possible to avoid potential problems, and to take advantage of material benefits. It also poses some knotty philosophical problems. If we could really see into the future, then our paths would be fixed; nothing we could do would affect the future, because we would have already seen it happen. But if we could see only one of several alternative futures, then we have the possibility of selecting the one which seems most favourable.

This is the approach adopted by most modern prophets. 'If you take a certain action, this is the probable result.' This makes it very difficult indeed to determine whether or not their prophecies are accurate, because the free will of the person involved can always act in a way not covered by the prophecy.

Premonitions are things which most people have at some time or other, and inevitably, these sometimes prove correct. But occasionally, people have a dream, or more rarely a waking vision, which depicts future events in a disturbingly clear way. These are not like the *déjà vu* sensation we all experience sometimes, when we have a momentary feeling that we have been in a certain situation before, or can anticipate the next few words of a conversation. The prophetic dream or vision is an obvious warning of some unpleasant event which is shortly going to take place, and is usually taken very seriously by the person experiencing it.

Fortune telling has a long history, but has now become little more than a parlour game. Reading tea leaves is a traditional method of divination, in which the random pattern of leaves on the bottom of the cup are interpreted by the 'reader', who sees 'pictures' in their shapes, rather like the Ink Blot test used in psychiatry. Like the crystal ball, or the black-glass mirror used by many more sophisticated fortune-tellers or mediums, tea leaves serve as a focus for the attention of the medium, letting imagination have a free rein.

▲ After the 66,000 ton *Titanic* sank on her maiden voyage, it was found that a number of people had experienced premonitions of the disaster, and saved their lives by cancelling their passages.

Generally, speaking, the more terrible the disaster, the more people report premonitions and warning dreams. Consequently, there are many instances of premonitions about the sinking of the Titanic, the crash of the airship R101, and for assassinations of famous political figures.

Aberfan

In 1966, in the Welsh mining village of Aberfan, an avalanche of black mud and coal dust slid down from a towering slag heap, and engulfed the village school and several houses. 116 children and 28 adults died in the tragedy. A survey made shortly afterwards showed that at least 76 people had quite clear premonitions of the disaster. And of these, 24 accounts were confirmed as having been reported to others *before* the disaster struck. At least two actually recorded their premonitions in writing before the event. Their ages varied widely; from 11 to 73 years of age, and by far the majority of people affected were women.

In general, these people reported sensa-

◄ Like the *Titanic*, the maiden voyage of the R101 ended in disaster. At least two of her crew are known to have had premonitions of their death in the crash; one other refused to fly in her, drove off on his motor cycle after the launching, and was killed in a road accident.

▲ When President Kennedy was assassinated in Dallas, the published premonitions of the American psychic Jeanne Dixon were vindicated in full. Some time later, she prophesied the death of his brother Robert, who was also murdered.

tions of choking and suffocation, and some experienced feelings of terror which in some cases were so severe that they were unable to continue their normal work. Most tragic of these was the little girl who had quite clear premonitions of her own death under the mountain of black mud.

This type of report is difficult to evaluate, because it is always made after the event, but recently, an attempt has been made to collect such premonitions together in advance, in order to see if they correlate with any later disaster.

The *Titanic*

In a few cases, it seems that a person can receive an extremely detailed premonition, without recognizing it as such. This was the case with the little-known author Morgan Robertson, who in 1898 wrote a prophetic novel entitled *The Wreck of the Titan*. In his book, the *Titan* was the world's largest liner, which struck an iceberg on her maiden voyage and sank, taking most of her 2,500 passengers with her. This huge death toll was due to the fact that the lifeboats of the

▼ The school in the small Welsh village of Aberfan was destroyed when a mountain of coal waste collapsed. One of the children foretold her own death.

In 1555, the prophet Nostradamus published a book of rhymed prophecies which have mystified the world ever since. The cryptic verses can be interpreted in such a way as to foretell the First and Second World Wars, the rise and fall of Hitler, the French Revolution, and the destruction of the entire world about the year 2,000 AD:

fictional liner could carry fewer than half of the passengers. Fourteen years later, the *Titanic* struck an iceberg on her maiden voyage, and took most of her passengers to the bottom with her, largely because of the inadequacy of her lifeboats. Several people had cancelled their passages because of their premonitions of disaster, and some of those who actually died are known to have told friends and relatives of their belief that something was going to happen.

Mass premonitions of this sort are not uncommon, and one researcher carried out a survey on the numbers of passengers carried on 28 trains which were involved in railway accidents. There were found to be significantly fewer passengers than usual on these trains, as though passengers had somehow avoided travelling by some mass premonition. In addition, the coaches damaged in the accidents also carried fewer than usual passengers.

Predicted assassinations

Notable premonitions were also associated with the murders of President John F. Kennedy and Robert Kennedy. A well-known American psychic, Jeanne Dixon, had a vivid premonition, back in 1952, that John Kennedy, then a relative unknown, would become president and be assassinated in office. Eleven years later, in Dallas, her prediction became completely fulfilled.

A few years later, in 1968, she remarked to an acquaintance that Martin Luther King would soon be shot, and that Robert Kennedy would be the next. A few days later, King was murdered. Later the same year, at a meeting in the Ambassador Hotel in Los Angeles, Jeanne Dixon predicted that Robert Kennedy would never become President, because of a tragedy which would befall him in that very same hotel. A week later, Kennedy was dead, killed by an assassin's bullet, in the Ambassador Hotel.

These premonitions are impressive, but should probably be treated with some caution. In the troubled world of American politics it is not too unlikely that any notable political figure might be assassinated. And of course, no one remembers the prophecies which did not come true.

Like many other manifestations of the paranormal, premonitions can only be studied effectively if such sweeping prophecies are ruled out, and small and unambiguous events are studied in the laboratory. In the modern parapsychology laboratory, the study of precognition involves subjects guessing which of a row of coloured lights will light up next, removing all doubts as to interpretation of the results obtained.

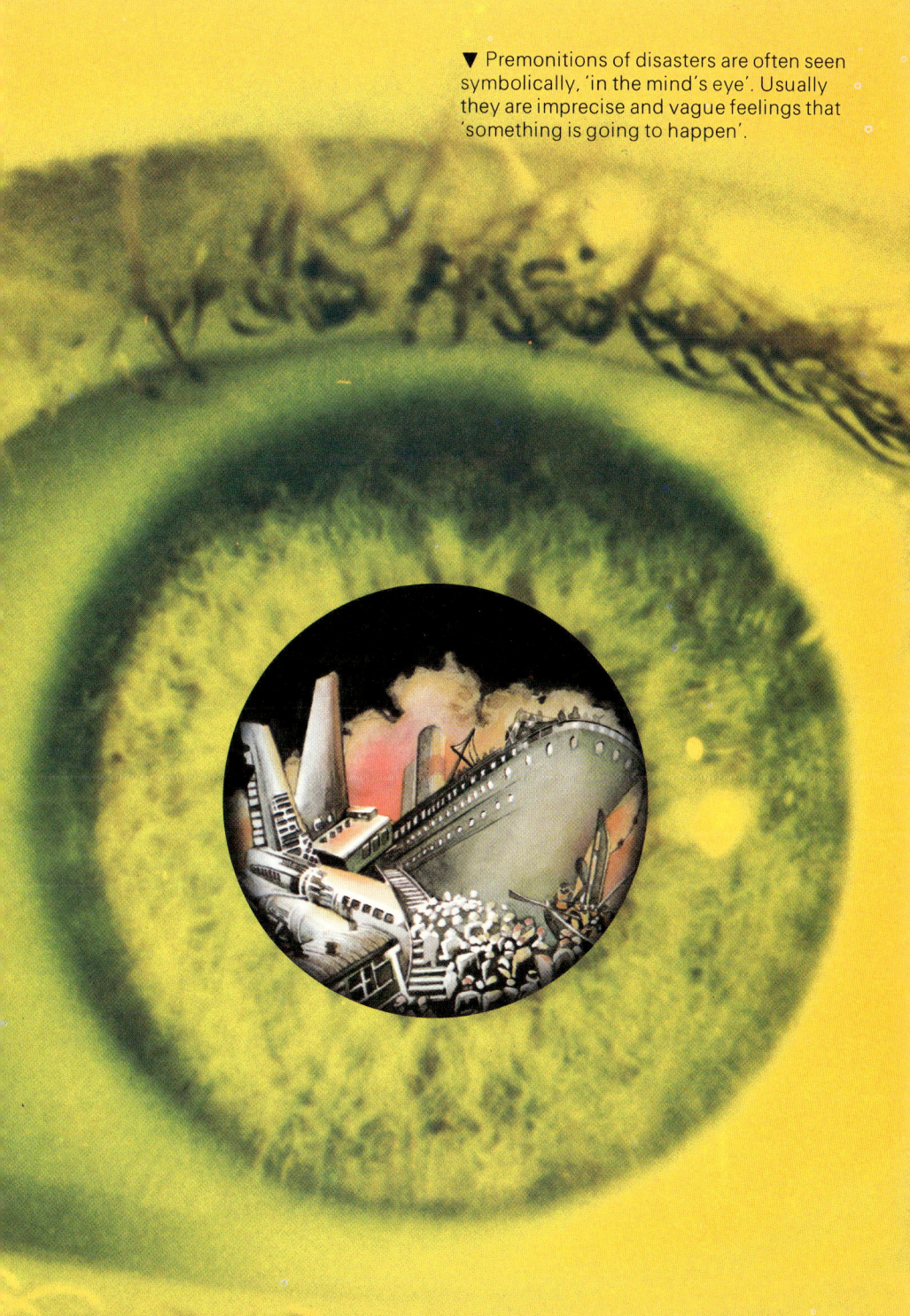

▼ Premonitions of disasters are often seen symbolically, 'in the mind's eye'. Usually they are imprecise and vague feelings that 'something is going to happen'.

Psychic prodigies

Of the many psychics and mediums who caught the imagination of the general public, probably the most respected was Daniel Dunglas Home, who has become famous as 'the medium who was never exposed'. Home was born in Scotland in 1833, and moved to the United States at an early age. Very soon after the Fox sisters began to produce their 'spirit rappings', Home began to conduct seances which proved so successful that he was invited to give demonstrations at the homes of the rich and the famous.

Because of the early date at which Home flourished, and of the circle of people for whom he gave demonstrations, he was never subjected to a scientific examination acceptable by modern standards, but nevertheless, Home repeatedly produced phenomena which are very difficult to explain by means of trickery.

The most astonishing feat he performed was levitation. Sometimes he would float in the air in a darkened seance room; on one occasion he was reported to have floated so high that his head touched the ceiling.

Home's repertoire

Home excelled at producing the physical phenomena which have now almost disappeared from the modern mediums' repertoire. At his seances, phantom hands appeared and floated in mid-air, sometimes

◀ D. D. Home was a Victorian medium who could reportedly levitate himself to a considerable height, and on one occasion, floated bodily out of one upstairs window, and in at the next.

▶ Home has become famous as one of the few mediums who was never exposed as a fraud. He was extremely scornful of his contemporaries who could only work in a darkened room or within a cabinet, from which they produced phantom hands and the like. Many of his feats are inexplicable even today.

tugging at the clothes of his audience. Musical instruments, such as an accordion, also floated about the seance room, playing as they did so. Tables tipped, and weird phantom rappings were heard all about the room.

Yet there was more to Home than the trickery used by many of his contemporaries. Home's spirit hands were tangible. They could be grasped by the sitters, and apparently were not simply wax or wood. Most disconcerting of all, even when a spirit hand was firmly grasped, it would literally evaporate from the grip of the sitter.

In addition to these typical seance-room phenomena, Home had another speciality. He could cause his body to elongate by about a foot, in broad daylight, and with hardly any possibility of trickery. This might have been a purely physical talent, but it is very difficult to see how it could have been done.

Mathew Manning

A young British psychic, Mathew Manning, seems likely to become even more famous than D. D. Home. Unlike many of his psychic predecessors, Manning is eager to have his powers investigated by qualified researchers, and has cooperated in a number of studies by psychologists. His abilities first became apparent when poltergeist phenomena began to afflict his home. At the time, he was 11 years old, and when psychic researchers were called in to investigate the strange movement of objects within closed rooms, Mathew was the obvious suspect. At first these events were confined to Mathew's home, and did not appear to affect his boarding school, but very soon, poltergeist phenomena began to disrupt the dormitories at school. Bunks were moved about, stones and other small objects appeared inexplicably, and strangest of all,

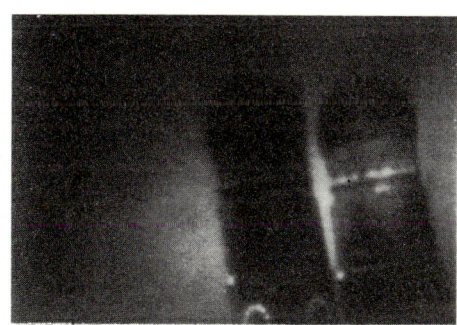

Ted Serios produces what he calls 'thoughtographs', by staring into the lens of a camera. The upper picture is one of his 'thoughtographs' produced in this way, while the one below is of his target, the towers of Franchen Kirche, in Munich. Serios' picture is from a viewpoint which cannot be reached normally. It has of course been suggested that he uses trickery, but evidence like this is very convincing. Serios produces his pictures after a period of deep concentration, after which he almost explodes with energy as he shouts 'Now' at his assistant, who clicks the shutter at that precise moment. He seems to know in advance if the picture has been successful.

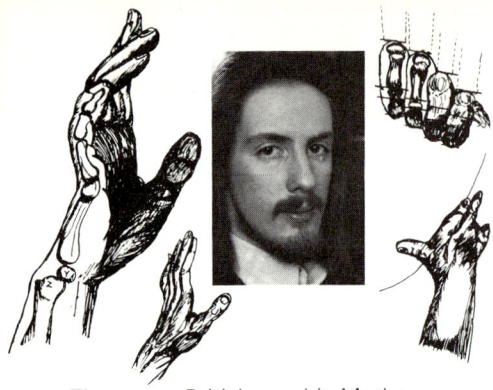

▲ The young British psychic Mathew Manning has produced huge quantities of automatic writing and drawings. These studies of hands, apparently the work of the artist Dürer, were made in the course of an hour, in 1971.

cold spots appeared in the room with no apparent cause, and in front of another witness, a patch of wall began to glow gently.

Shortly after this incident, Mathew began to receive 'spirit communications', both in the form of mental voices, and as automatic writing. The written communications predominated, and many of the messages received were apparently from people who had died violently or unpleasantly. Some had died quite recently, others had lived as far back as Elizabethan times.

Over the years, Mathew Manning produced a huge quantity of automatic writing. Much of this could be related to the person with whom Mathew was apparently communicating. Both the handwriting and the

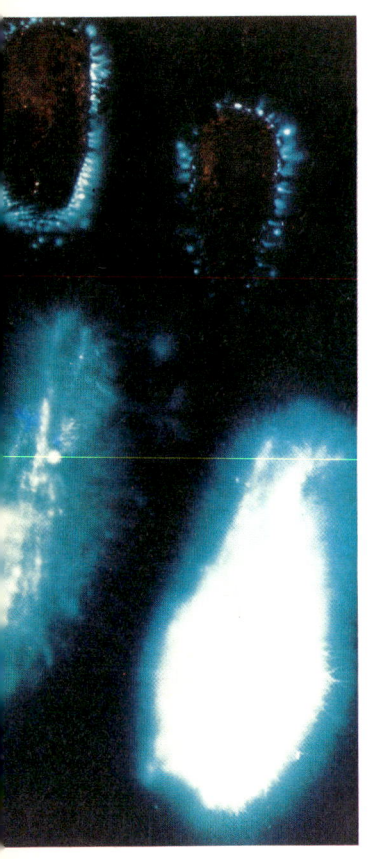

content of the messages was often recognizably in the style of well-known figures of the past. Messages were received from Bertrand Russell, and even from Mrs Beeton, the founder of the famous cookery book. Many of the communications were in foreign languages, including Russian, Greek, and even Saxon and Old English. Some were in Arabic, and these confounded a Professor from the American University at Beirut, who found that the script ranged from that of an almost illiterate hand to that of an expert calligrapher.

Mathew now began to produce automatic drawings of a very high quality. These appeared to be the work of artists such as Picasso, Matisse, Beardsley, Dürer, and many others.

Research on Mathew Manning has yielded some valuable clues to the workings of the mind of a psychic. When he was connected to an EEG machine, which measured his brain waves, and asked to 'switch his power on', an unprecedented reading was obtained. According to the machine, Mathew was producing powerful bursts of psychic energy in the theta range; that is, the type of brain waves produced when someone is deep in sleep. Yet Mathew was quite obviously awake at the time. The power of the readings was the highest ever recorded.

◀ *Far left*. The new technique of Kirlian photography is often said to show the aura, which is particularly marked in psychics. In the top part of this illustration, Mathew Manning's normal Kirlian 'fingerprint' is shown, while in the ones below, he had been asked to 'turn on the power'.

◀ *Left*. An automatic drawing by Mathew Manning depicting Queen Elizabeth I, and purportedly drawn by a spirit called Isaac Oliver.

Uri Geller

Another major psychic of our time is Uri Geller, the controversial Israeli who has appeared on television many times, demonstrating his ability to bend spoons and other pieces of metal, apparently by the power of his mind. Geller's ability to bend metal by stroking it gently is now very well known. It is unfortunately very difficult to test this ability, especially if the psychic subject holds the object he is attempting to bend, since the possibility of fraudulently substituting a pre-bent piece of metal or of

▲ Uri Geller, a psychic now famous throughout the world for his metal-bending.

bending it by manual means cannot be completely eliminated.

However, metallurgists have examined some of the test pieces bent or broken by Geller, and in some cases, they are unable to provide an explanation for the changes in the microscopic structure of the specimens.

Another of Geller's specialities is to reproduce on paper drawings made previously by another person, and subsequently sealed securely in an envelope. Geller usually handles the envelope for a while,

▼ The target (1) and the response (2) in an ESP trial with Geller, carried out at Stanford Research Institute. There is an almost exact match.

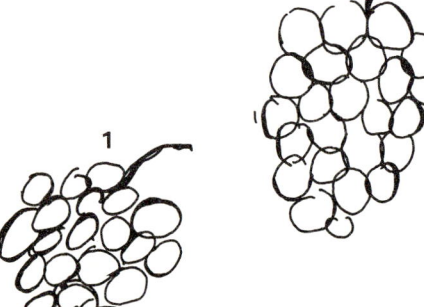

doodling on a pad of paper as he does so. His answer is sometimes an exact copy of the target drawing, or more often, a near miss which makes it very difficult to decide whether or not his psychic powers are operating. Some of these misses are themselves very interesting, however. In response to a drawing, he may produce a word describing the target, or a drawing which is of a different object, but with a similar shape to that of the target.

On one occasion, his target was a drawing of a bridge. Geller drew a bridge, but his was of the hump-backed variety, while the target drawing was of a suspension bridge.

It is probably fair to say that none of the experiments done with Geller have absolutely excluded fraud. Many of his critics claim that he is simply a very skilled stage magician, and indeed, most of his feats have been duplicated by magicians, who in some cases have hoodwinked psychic researchers to demonstrate the ease with which they can be deceived.

This does not mean that Geller is a fraud, but simply that no one has yet designed experiments which are completely proof against all forms of tampering. For example, one of Uri Geller's most impressive demonstrations was to produce strange peaks in the graph drawn by a Geiger counter in the laboratory. But Randi, a stage magician, claimed to be able to produce the same effect—not by emitting bursts of radiation, but by jarring the floor near the recording machine, and causing the recording pen to wobble.

▲ Along with many other youngsters, seven-year old Mark Shelley is an accomplished spoon-bender.

▼ After Geller's televised appearances many other people came forward, claiming to have similar powers. Some of these are now being investigated at London University.

Psychic frauds

Any serious consideration of the paranormal is hindered by accusations of fraud and trickery. To a committed sceptic, the paranormal is, and will always remain a total impossibility. This means that any positive results obtained must be the results of either sloppy experiments, fraudulent psychic subjects, or self-delusion on the part of the experimenter. Unfortunately, the sceptics have much past history to back them up, although modern researchers have done much to overcome the deficiencies of earlier work.

Fraudulent mediums have been with us ever since men first began to commune with the spirits, back in the dawn of history. They first sprang to popular attention with the advent of modern spirit mediums in the latter part of the 19th century. It was all too easy to trick people who wanted to believe in life after death.

At this time, many mediums worked in a darkened room. Some mediums grouped their sitters about a table. The medium and the sitters generally placed their hands upon the table, while the medium went into a trance and began to speak in the voices of the spirits. All around them in the gloom, the physical manifestations of the seance room would take place.

Ectoplasm—wraith or rag?

Much of the fraud centred about the alleged production of a paranormal life essence called 'ectoplasm'. During the seance, with the medium deep in a trance, this cloudy white substance would apparently emerge from the medium's mouth, nose, or other apertures of the body. Drifting through the curtains surrounding

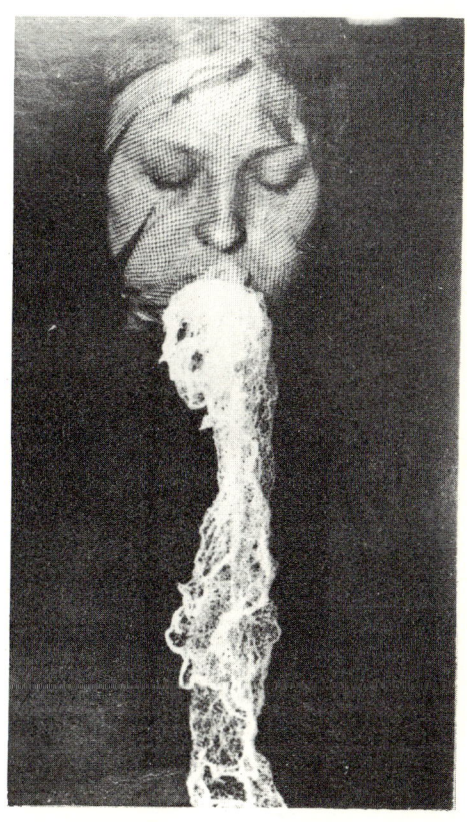

▲ Ectoplasm was an insubstantial substance produced by mediums deep in trance, which apparently solidified into recognizable shapes, and even into complete 'spirits'. Sometimes it appeared to be gauze or muslin, which had been concealed in the medium's mouth.

the cabinet, the ectoplasm gradually condensed into a recognizable human form; either the medium's spirit guide, or a recognizable face from among the departed relatives of members of the audience.

The advent of serious psychic research,

and more particularly, of the flash photograph, put an end to much of this type of manifestation. It is true to say that there were some well authenticated cases of mediums manifesting ectoplasm, but more often than not the ectoplasm turned out to be muslin or cheesecloth, or sometimes even paper. This was ingeniously concealed by the medium, then gradually unrolled to reveal a painted face.

Eusapia Palladino

The type of medium who sat at the seance table, surrounded by keenly interested sitters, was a much more skilful practitioner of her arts. Of these, the Italian medium Eusapia Palladino reigned supreme. Eusapia could levitate tables, produce spirit rappings, spirit hands, and most of the other common manifestations of the time.

But unlike most of her contemporaries, Eusapia Palladino submitted herself many times to rigorous scientific testing.

For quite some time she had eminent members of the British Society for Psychical Research convinced that for once, they had found the genuine article. The SPR had evolved techniques for controlling the movements of the medium in a darkened room. On one side, a sitter grasped her wrist, and placed one foot on top of her shoe to immobilize her leg. On her other side, Eusapia's hand rested on the hand of another sitter, whose foot was similarly placed over her shoe.

This was not sufficient to prevent the table rising bodily into the air, and taps and other odd noises from sounding about the room. It was quite some time before they

▼ In the darkened seance room, the unprincipled medium found it easy to cause musical instruments to float about, and spirit hands to tug at the clothes of the sitters.

▼ Even if the medium's feet were held down, it was generally possible for her to slip her feet out of her shoes, and use the freed foot to levitate the table or produce spirit rappings.

found how she caused some of these effects, while working in the dark. Gradually moving her hands closer together, she was able to leave one hand resting on that of an investigator, while the other sitter grasped the same hand about the wrist. Her other hand was now free to work miracles. And so were her feet, for they also found that her feet could be easily slid from within her hard-capped boots, leaving the sitter's own feet confidently holding the empty boots in place. By lifting firmly with outstretched legs—up went the table. Although it was proved she cheated when she had the chance it was never proved that *all* her feats were spurious. On balance it seems possible that she did have astonishing psychic talents.

With hindsight, some manifestations produced by fraudulent mediums may seem simply amusing, but at the time they were actually very cruelly playing on the emotions of bereaved people, and deriving a good income from it.

Later frauds, or suspected frauds, have no obvious motive, other than a desire to 'prove' the validity of paranormal phenomena. Modern researchers have been accused of altering the score cards during ESP tests, of using poorly shuffled Zener cards, and even of peering through skylights to watch the Zener cards being turned over. In most of these tests it would actually only require a very small 'adjustment' of the results to make them statistically significant, but it is difficult to imagine such a fraud taking place on an international scale. Indeed, this 'normal' explanation is much more unlikely than the existence of the paranormal.

▼ Investigators went to considerable lengths to imobilize the mediums. The mediums proved equally industrious at finding ways of evading the controls, and continued to produce amazing effects.

▼ A hair stretched across the balance pan of a sensitive scale provided proof of the weight of ectoplasm. Spirit draughts and spirit music were, for the experienced medium, equally easy to conjure up.

The psychic significance of dreams

There is much evidence to show that ESP is most likely to occur while we are in an altered state of consciousness. This simply means that the mind is operating on a level different from that on which we conduct our day-to-day life. It has been demonstrated that ESP often occurs when we are in a relaxed yet alert state; it can also occur when in a state of nervous tension. Many apparent cases of ESP occur when a person is in that half-conscious state just before drifting off to sleep, or in a half-awake mood just after sleeping. These are all examples of altered states of consciousness, as is hypnosis, which is known to be of considerable importance in enhancing ESP ability.

Most important of all of these altered states of consciousness is sleep itself, when our imaginations run riot and are expressed in the form of dreams. If, as is often suggested, our weak facility for ESP is usually suppressed by the conscious mind, it is reasonable to suppose that it might manifest itself in the form of dreams. Indeed, it has long been known that many trains of thought which we do not usually allow ourselves to pursue can erupt into our consciousness in the form of disturbing dreams, although their meaning is usually heavily veiled. Interpretation of dreams is an important part of psychoanalysis, although followers of different schools of psychiatry have widely conflicting views on what they mean.

Prophetic dreams

Some dreams are quite explicit in their meaning, however, and these are often prophetic. One well known example was reported by Mark Twain, who had a clear dream of his brother's body lying in a metal coffin supported across two chairs, and

▶ According to Freud, most of the symbols we see in dreams have a sexual meaning. Apples, for example (1), represent breasts, and various types of shells (2), and the open door (3) stand for the vagina. The room within (4) represents the womb, and this is unlocked by the key (5). The symbols for the penis are many and varied. The snake (6), watering can (7) and tower (8) are obvious. The diver (9) represents penetration, water (11) means birth and royalty (12) means parents.

with a bouquet of white and crimson flowers resting on his chest. Only a few weeks later, his brother was killed when a riverboat boiler exploded, and when Twain saw the body, he found it laid out exactly as the dream had foreseen, in a metal coffin supported on chairs. While he watched, a woman entered the room and placed a bouquet of white flowers, containing a single crimson bloom, on his dead brother's chest.

Dream ESP differs from waking experiences in that the information received tends to be more complete. However, because it *is* information received in a dream, many people are able to dismiss apparent warnings as simple nightmares. On the other hand, there is some evidence that it is possible to alter the course of events forecast in a prophetic dream. If this is true, it means that prophetic dreams are not truly revealing the future, but only showing the future as it could be if we follow a particular course of action.

Dream experiments

The study of dreams offers great possibilities for important advances in the study of the paranormal, and some very advanced techniques have been evolved to allow dreams to be studied in detail.

We all dream several times each night, when the body goes into a peculiar state called paradoxical sleep. When this occurs, our eyes move about rapidly beneath closed eyelids, while our body becomes completely limp. If a person is woken during this Rapid Eye Movement or REM sleep, they will find that their dream has been interrupted, and that much of it can be recalled. Otherwise, they will drift into normal dreamless sleep, and experience several more cycles of dreaming and non-dreaming sleep before waking naturally with little or no recollection of the intense mental activity of the previous night.

This situation can be exploited by the parapsychologist. In the Maimonides Dream

▲ Salvador Dali's painting, 'The outskirts of paranoia', like many of his other works, contain ambiguous and symbolic elements characteristic of dreams.

Laboratory in New York, volunteers slept in the laboratory, while their physical and mental states were carefully monitored. In another room or building, anything between 20 and 70 km away from the dreaming subject, one of the experimenters concentrated on a picture selected at random from a number chosen for their emotional content or interest. It was hoped that this would overcome the falling-off of scores usually found in experiments involving Zener cards, which is thought to result from boredom due to the neutral nature of the symbols shown on the cards.

At the end of each period of dreaming the subject was woken and questioned as to the content of the dream.

In some of the experiments, the 'sender' was given more stimuli associated with the picture, in the hope that the ESP message which resulted would be stronger. These might be sequences of coloured slides, music, or objects which the sender handled.

Transmitting dreams

A further series of tests of precognitive or prophetic dreams were made, where the subjects were asked to try and dream about an event in which they would be involved. In both these series of tests, independent judges were asked to match the dreamers' responses to the targets, in order to eliminate any bias on the part of the experimenters.

The results were some of the most convincing evidence ever obtained for the existence of ESP, and better still, in some cases they were able to repeat previous experiments and obtain similar results—which is very rare in the study of the temperamental phenomena of parapsychology.

Laboratory tests

In other dream laboratories, the experimenters took a different approach, attempting to find out what would happen if both sender *and* receiver were asleep. Could one transmit his dream to the other? A subject was given an hypnotic suggestion that he dream of Martin Luther King and of riots. He actually dreamed of King's murder; someone had thrown a rock, and rioting was feared.

The other subject, without any hypnotic prompting, dreamed that a negro policeman was beating up another man. He feared that someone would throw a brick and precipitate a riot. Similar corresponding dreams were obtained in other tests, although none were so close to the target as to definitely prove that ESP was operating.

Because dream research allows the experimenters to know exactly *when* their subjects are likely to experience ESP, it allows more meaningful experimental results to be obtained. The long and tedious sets of guesses which are necessary to demonstrate a slight possibility of ESP when using Zener cards can be avoided, and with the aid of hypnosis, the paranormal faculty can probably be enhanced.

> Do you sometimes feel as though you had just fallen a few inches onto the bed, while you are on the point of drifting off to sleep? This sensation, which can be quite frightening, is called a myoclonic jerk, and results from the sudden discharge of electrical energy in the brain, like a very small epileptic fit. However, it is perfectly normal and happens to everyone periodically. Some people have more definite feelings of being levitated while they sleep, and have even claimed to have found themselves floating near the ceiling. This is probably better explained as a form of travelling clairvoyance or OOBE, rather than true levitation. Full-blown OOBE's do occur during dreaming, and one of the most dramatic was the case of a woman in the USA who visited her husband in an OOBE, while he was on a transatlantic liner. Another occupant of his stateroom actually *saw* her, and this witnesses' description, the husband's testimony, and the wife's own account of her OOBE all tallied precisely.

▶ In the modern dream laboratory, subjects spend several nights sleeping under strictly controlled conditions. Electrodes attached to their scalps monitor the electrical activity of their brains, while the experimenter concentrates on a telepathic target which he tries to send to his sleeping subject.

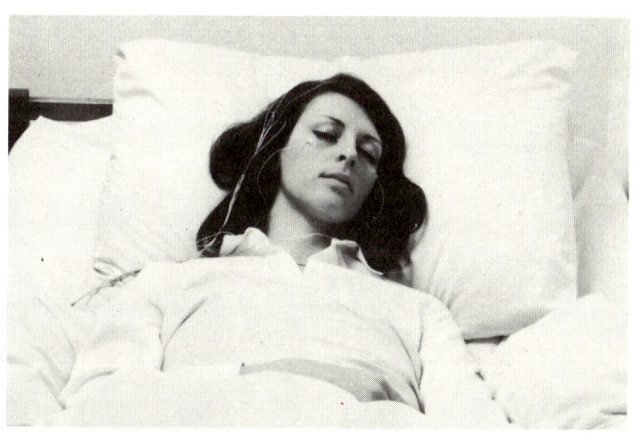

Animal ESP

Most people who have kept pets will have noticed the almost incredible degree to which an animal learns to anticipate its master's actions. The pet cat will run out into the kitchen just as you decide it's time to feed it. The dog presents itself at the front door in anticipation of its master's return, but before it can possibly hear his car approaching. The uncanny ability of a sheepdog to work with the shepherd is legendary. Are these paranormal abilities, or are the senses of animals so superior to those of man that they just seem inexplicable?

There have been a number of cases of 'educated' animals which demonstrate just how sensitive their normal senses can be. Horses, dogs, pigs, and even geese have given demonstrations of 'mind reading', giving the answers to questions by spelling out simple codes with foot tappings, or by picking out cards. But they have always failed when their masters were not present, and it seems obvious that they were actually picking up imperceptible and probably involuntary cues from their masters. The 'talking' horses, for example, could also count very well. They tapped their hoof steadily, until they reached the desired number, when an almost unnoticeable movement of their master told them when to stop. Letters could be tapped out in the same way, or instructions be given as to the correct card to select.

Other cases of apparent ESP are quite inexplicable; the case of a wild dolphin, for example, which befriended a skin diver off the Isle of Man, and disappeared after several weeks. Some time later, while the man was diving 300km away off the Pembroke coast, the same dolphin appeared alongside the boat, and welcomed him in the water. The odds against this type of chance are impossible to compute.

The Chinese consider the 'sixth sense' of animals reliable enough to make it an integral part of their system for forecasting earthquakes, although whether this is a form of animal precognition, or whether minute tremors can be heard by animals and affect their behaviour accordingly is not clear.

Laboratory tests

In the laboratory, some promising results have been obtained in animal ESP studies. In many ways, these experiments have more to offer than do experiments with human subjects, as they can be repeated as often as required, with almost unlimited numbers of subjects. Most are quite simple experiments to conduct. For example, mice, gerbils, or hamsters can be placed in a cage with the floor divided into two sections. At random, a mild electric shock is delivered through one or other half of the floor. If the animal is capable of precognition, it will be able to avoid the shock by jumping into the opposite side of the cage. In fact, these experiments have shown, remarkably consistently, that small rodents do have some talent for precognition.

Animals have also been used in trials on PK, or psychokinetic ability. Using radioactive random number generators (discussed more fully in the next chapter) which controlled the amount of time that heating lamps were on in the experimental area, it was found that cats, lizards and chicks could all apparently vary the amount of time the light stayed on. And so, more controversially, could fertile eggs, although unfertilized eggs scored no better than chance would predict. In a similar experiment using cockroaches which were given electric shocks, it was found that they received significantly *more* shocks than predicted—with odds of as much as 8,000 to 1 against chance.

Stories of dogs following their masters over long distances are common, and one of the most recent was the case of 'Bede', an English Setter, who travelled 300 miles from Cornwall to Essex in order to find his master.

Animal navigation

Homing behaviour and animal navigation are well known abilities of a wide range of animals. Birds, turtles, salmon and eels all carry out migrations for enormous distances, unerringly finding their way to their destination. In the case of salmon, they return to the actual rivulet in which they were hatched. Many ingenious sug-

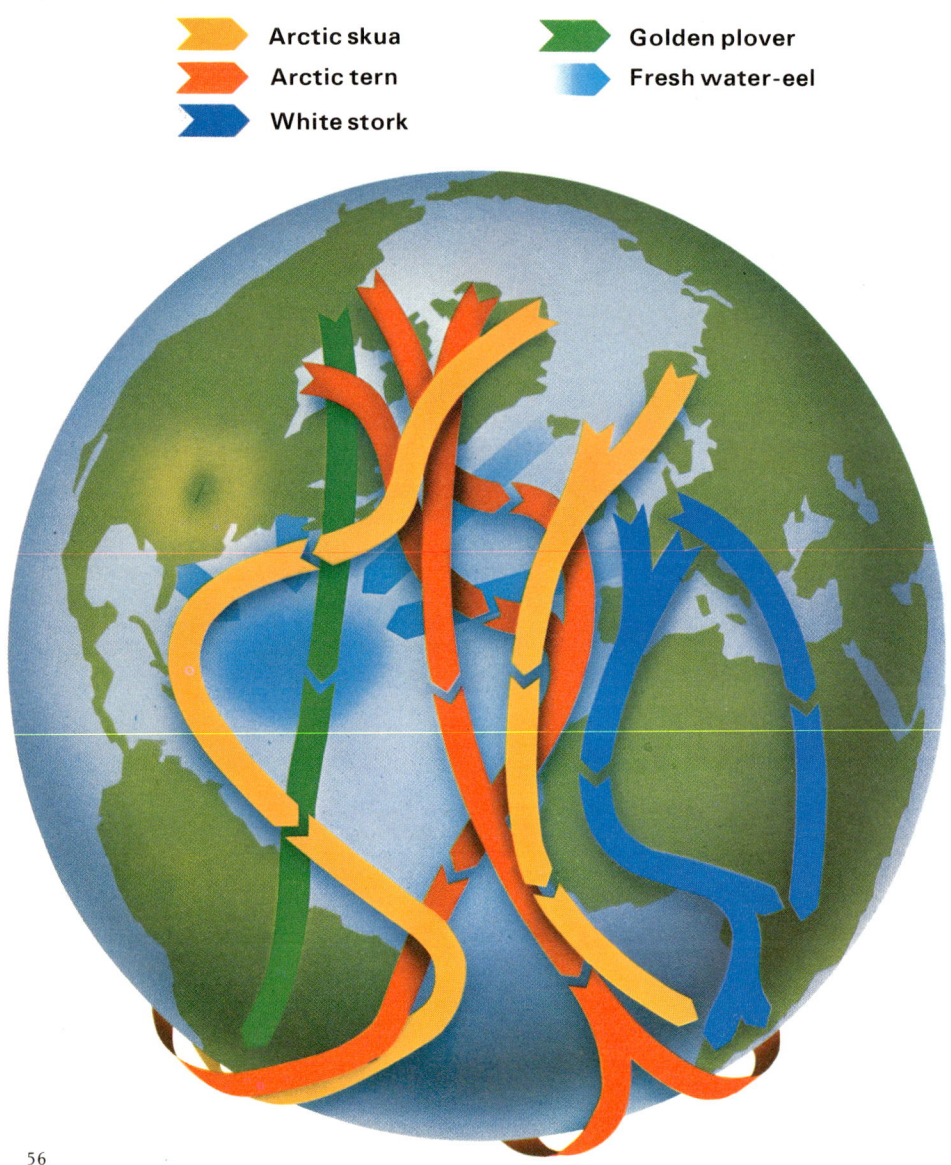

BIRD AND EEL MIGRATION ROUTES
- Arctic skua
- Arctic tern
- White stork
- Golden plover
- Fresh water-eel

gestions have been made to explain these feats, such as orientation by means of the earth's magnetic field, by polarized sunlight, or by celestial navigation like that carried out by sailors with the aid of a sextant. But whenever experiments have been set up to exclude these methods of navigation, the animals still seem to find their way to their destination. Even with frosted contact lenses fitted, pigeons have managed to find their way home.

Psi-trailing is even more baffling. This is the well known ability of dogs and cats to find their way to their masters or to their old homes over hundreds of kilometres distant. Cats are particularly good at finding their old home after their household has moved to another area, in the same way that pigeons return to their loft, but it is difficult to think of any alternative to ESP when a dog finds its master in totally unfamiliar territory.

▲ Animals seem to have strong premonitions of disaster. Rats and other animals know when an earthquake is to strike, and maybe actually do leave a 'sinking ship' before the event.

◄ With a simple testing cage, experiments in animal precognition can be automated. Either side of this cage can be electrified to produce a mild shock, which the animal can avoid by jumping over the low barrier. As it does so it breaks a light beam, which records its position in the cage. A random number generator determines which side will become live next, so the experimenter need take no active part at all. It was found that mice did avoid going into the side of the cage to which the shock was going to be delivered, much more frequently than one would expect by chance alone. The odds against chance were over 1,000 to one.

Parascience

After the 1930s, study of the phenomena of the paranormal took place broadly along the lines established by Rhine and his contemporaries. Most experiments sought very small statistically significant deviations from the results predicted by chance. But at the end of the 1960s, Western researchers became aware of a different type of research being carried out in Russia and other Iron Curtain countries. These experiments apparently produced physical phenomena reminiscent of those seen in the heyday of spirit mediums. The medium Nelya Mikhailova caused small objects to roll about the surface of a table, and a compass needle to spin dizzily. Other psychic subjects conducted telepathy experiments over huge distances, with very reliable results, and a unique form of 'psychic' photography was developed.

At first, these experiments did not unduly impress Western researchers. The Russians did not have the long history of experimentation into the paranormal which their Western colleagues could draw on. Their experiments were not often repeatable; one dramatic success was enough to convince the Russians that they had a valid result. But before long, the Russians and their fellow-workers were producing impressive results backed up by more detailed observations. In particular, they concentrated on the intensive monitoring of the physiological states of their psychic subjects, measuring brain activity, blood pressure, and a range of other functions.

Telepathic morse

One such experiment involved long-distance telepathy between Moscow and Leningrad. In Leningrad, the psychic Nicolaiev was wired into an EEG machine which recorded his brain waves. 550km away in Moscow, the sender Kamensky attempted to send a message in Morse code, in the form of bursts of telepathic emotional energy. To generate the 'psychic energy' required, Kamensky imagined himself physically attacking Nicolaiev, in bursts of 15 seconds for a 'dot', and 45 seconds for a 'dash'. In Moscow, Nicolaiev noted the timing of each psychic attack, and his impressions were confirmed by the EEG reading, which demonstrated that at the same time, his brain waves were changing. In this way, the Russian word *mig* was spelled out, meaning 'instant'.

Following a lead from a Czech researcher, Douglas Dean in America carried out similar studies. Dean's work depended on the discovery that in many people, the blood volume changes very slightly when a person with whom they are emotionally connected thinks of their name. We are not normally conscious of this small change in blood volume, but it can be measured with an instrument called a plethysmograph. Using this machine, a simple code was worked out, which allowed Morse messages to be sent from as far as New York to Florida.

Psychic photography

Photography has long been a tool of psychic researchers, and took a new direction with the revelation that Ted Serios, a Chicago hotel worker, could produce pictures on photographic emulsion simply by thinking at the camera.

▶ Instrumentation has transformed modern psychic research, by allowing automatic recording of events and experiences. The flash camera (1), and infra-red camera (2) allow a visual record to be made of seances conducted in darkness. With a tape-recorder (3), a precise record of a medium's pronouncements can be made. Similarly, draughts produced by 'spirits' can be recorded (4), and other machines (5) measure temperature changes and alterations in the earth's magnetic field.

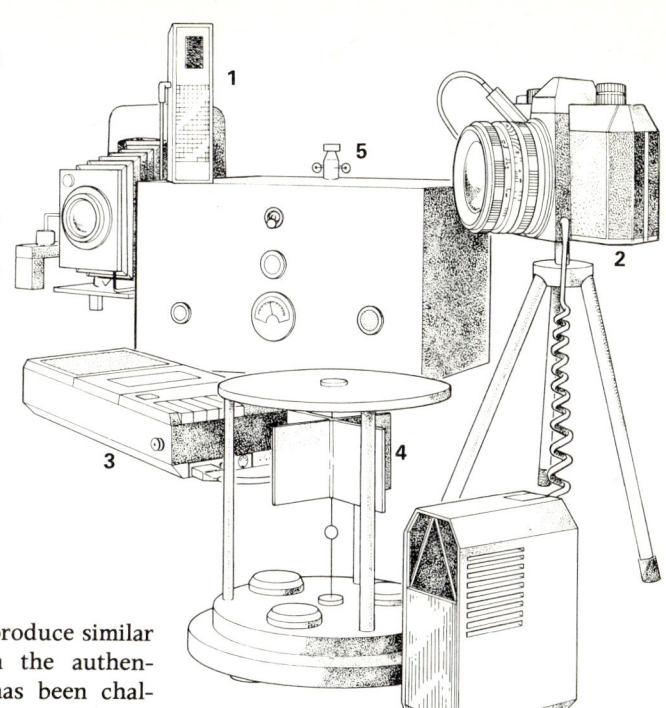

Uri Geller has managed to produce similar 'thoughtographs', although the authenticity of the phenomena has been challenged by sceptics who believe that the method is wide open to deliberate cheating.

A rather different type of photography has been developed by the Soviet scientist Semyon Kirlian, which relies on a novel method of producing an image. In Kirlian photography, no camera is used. Instead, the object to be photographed is sandwiched between two metal plates, resting against a sheet of colour film. An electrical potential is applied between the two plates, oscillating at a rate of as much as 200,000 cycles per second. When the film is developed, an image of the object appears, surrounded by startling plumes of coloured lights, and tiny twinkling patterns. A similar effect is obtained when a finger is pressed against film resting on the charged metal plate. These strange and beautiful effects are known to be associated with the corona effect; the electrical phenomenon which causes the Aurora Borealis or Northern Lights, and the glowing balls of light caused by St Elmo's fire, sometimes seen during a thunderstorm.

The exotic Kirlian effect has some unique applications, however. The colour of the plumes of light produced was found to vary, depending on the emotional state of the person whose finger rested on the film. Drugs, alchohol, excitement, and psychiatric disorder all seemed to produce distinctive variations in the traces obtained.

Working with a healer called Ethel de Loach, an American researcher demonstrated that the normal blue streamers of light obtained when she was resting normally turned into a vivid orange glow as soon as she exerted her healing powers.

Kirlian photography offers an exciting opportunity for research, as it automatically records the normally ephemeral phenomena of the paranormal, in a way not susceptible to the normal charges of cheating.

Tests of inanimate objects rather than people have yielded some baffling results which still defy explanation. Some of the earliest experiments were carried out on leaves, which were sandwiched between the metal plates of the Kirlian apparatus, and produced some quite remarkable pictures. It was soon found that virus diseases of plants, which are at an early stage quite undetectable by normal means, could be identified as patches or discolourations showing up on the photograph. Later results were even more surprising. Kirlian found that if a small portion of leaf was cut away before the photograph was made, sometimes a 'ghost' image of the missing portion could be seen in the picture, as though some part of the leaf still lingered in an invisible form. Western researchers were unable to repeat this experiment for several years, but after many attempts, some laboratories have produced similar phantom images.

It has been suggested that Kirlian photography reveals electrical fields around the living body, reminiscent of the aura which some occultists claim to be able to detect. Other scientists prefer more mundane explanations, pointing out that finger pressure on the photographic film can vary the colour of the image obtained, as can the amount of perspiration on the finger, and the skin temperature of the subject. The latest research is aimed at eliminating these variable factors, and at perfecting apparatus which will allow continuous recordings of the flares and plumes of light, rather than the single pictures obtained previously.

Psychotronic generators

In Czechoslovakia, Robert Pavlita claims to have invented devices which allow the

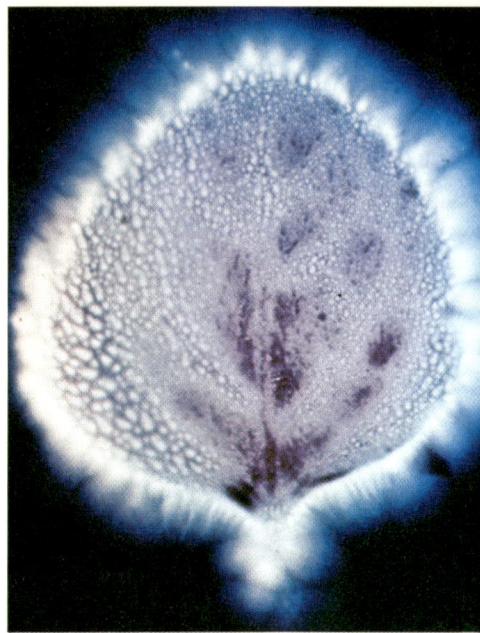

psychic power of the body to be focused in such a way that PK can readily be demonstrated. His 'Pavlita Generators' are small devices constructed from steel, brass, and other substances, with no apparent 'works'. Pavlita 'charges' one of his generators by simply concentrating on it, or touching it briefly against his head, after which it is ready to produce remarkable PK phenomena. Using his generators, Pavlita has caused a needle balanced on a pivot to rotate rapidly, picked up non-magnetic substances as though they were attracted to a powerful magnet, increased the rate of growth of plants, and purified specimens of polluted water. Although Pavlita Generators are now marketed outside the Iron Curtain countries, so far few people have reported similar successes.

Emotional plants

In spite of these dramatic reports, Russia and the other Iron Curtain countries have

◀ Photographed by Kirlian photography, a living leaf produces an image surrounded by a glowing halo, and covered with glittering points of light.

▶ This site engineer is using a commercially available set of dowsing rods to locate pipes and cables buried beneath the ground.

▼ When part of the leaf is cut away, occasionally a faint glowing 'ghost' of the leaf can be seen.

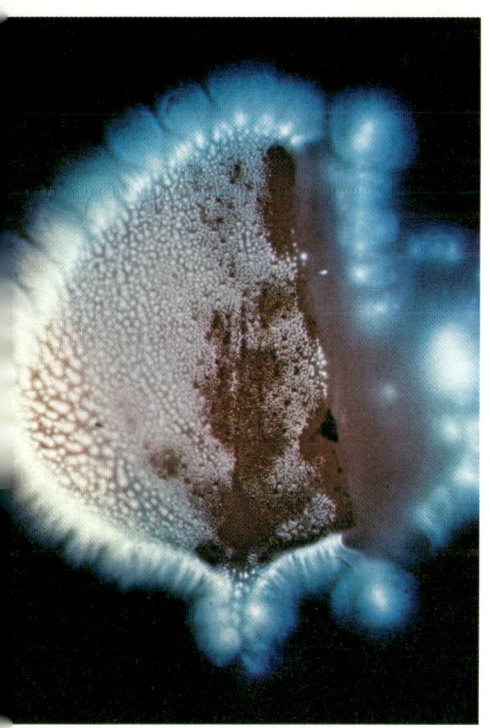

no monopoly on the more extreme forms of psychic phenomena. In America, Cleve Backster published the results of some experiments which defied logical explanation. Backster is an ex-CIA man, now running a school for police operators of polygraph machines, or lie detectors. One day he wired up a house plant to the electrodes of a polygraph, hoping to measure changes in water content of the plant, rather than the electrical resistance of skin, which is the usual function of the machine. For some reason he decided to try 'torturing' the plant, and dipped one of its leaves into hot coffee, producing no reaction on the machine. Then he thought of trying to burn a leaf more thoroughly with a match. At that moment, the polygraph responded violently, producing an upward 'blip' in the trace drawn by the recording pen. To test this apparent sensitivity, Backster experimented by dropping live brine shrimps into boiling water. The plant responded by producing a polygraph response each time one died, but made no response at all when dead shrimps were used. As a further refinement, Backster automated the apparatus, so that shrimps were dropped into the boiling water at random intervals. The plant still gave the same response.

In further tests, Backster used an 'accomplice' who 'murdered' another plant by uprooting it and breaking it up thoroughly. Thereafter, his wired-up plant recognized the 'murderer', and reacted violently every time he came into the same room.

More recently, Backster has demonstrated that other forms of simple life have the same ability. Fruit and vegetables, yeast, microbes, blood cells, and even cells scraped from the roof of the mouth all showed some degree of sensitivity to damage being caused to other forms of life.

Not surprisingly, researchers were unwilling to take this work seriously unless it could be duplicated elsewhere, and very few such repeat experiments have met with success. Another American, Paul Sauvin, found that he could obtain similar results with plants, and fitted up leaves with sensitive switches, which he found could be triggered simply by 'thinking at' the plant. The film director Fritz Lang made a documentary of Sauvin's plants in action. A psychic subject sent Morse code messages from San Francisco to Sauvin's plants in New York, the response being recorded on a filmed oscilloscope screen.

Bizarre though these experiments may seem, they arouse sufficient interest in the scientific world for 7,000 scientists to request reprints of the article in which Backster first published his results, and for at least two dozen American universities to announce their intention of repeating the experiment.

The machines of parascience

In more recent years, parapsychology in the Soviet Union has come in for some severe official criticism, and one of the leading researchers has been imprisoned. Other parapsychologists have fled to the West, and are continuing their work. In most of Europe and America, however, research continues along more traditional lines. The greatest advances have been the almost universal adoption of automated machines for the investigation of ESP and PK. The most widely used of these are the Schmidt machines, which produce their random targets by means of the most un-

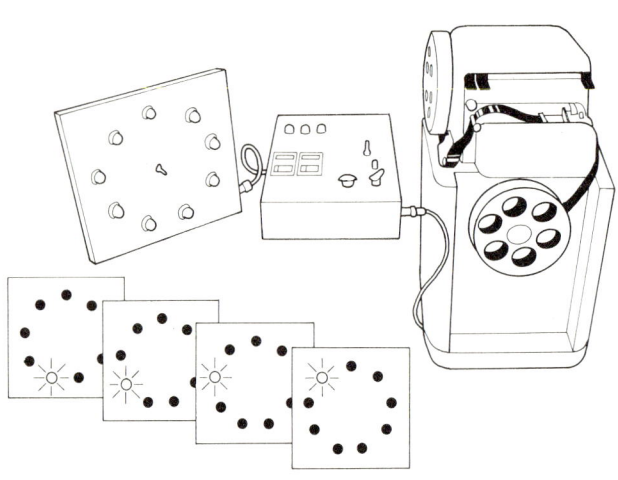

◀ The Schmidt PK testing machine relies on one of the most random events known to select its next target. The subject attempts, using PK powers, to force the circle of indicator lamps to light, one at a time, in a pre-determined direction.

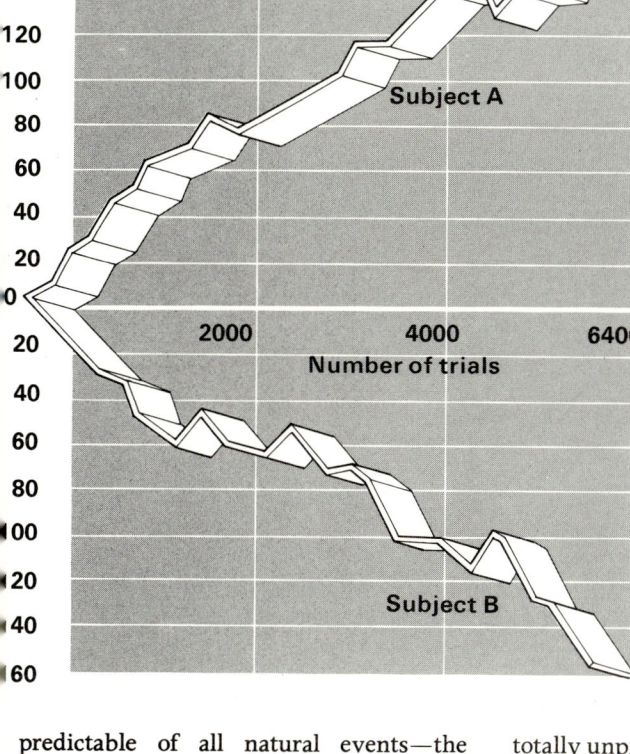

◀ Using the Schmidt machine, several subjects have been able to force the circle of lamps to light up in a regular sequence. Sometimes the results are not quite as intended. In these two tests, one subject managed to make the lights move in the specified direction. With the other subject, they lit up in the opposite direction to that which was intended. This is called PK missing, and is just as important a proof of paranormal events as the first test.

predictable of all natural events—the moment when a particle of radioactive Strontium 90 emits an electron.

There are two basic types of Schmidt machine. That used for tests of precognition has a bank of four indicator lamps, and the subject has to press a button beneath the lamp he thinks will be the next to light. His response is recorded automatically, eliminating any posibility of cheating. The mechanism is quite simple. Associated with the radioactive source is an electronic counter which counts up to four, then repeats itself endlessly, at a rate of a million digits per second. When an electron is emitted from the Strontium 90 source, it stops the counter, and depending on which stage in its four-digit cycle it has reached, will light up one of the four lamps, in a totally unpredictable manner.

In the Schmidt PK machine, a similar mechanism drives a circular display of indicator lamps. These lamps operate in a series of steps, one at a time, the next lamp lighting up in either a clockwise or anti-clockwise direction, depending on where the counting mechanism happens to come to rest when triggered by the next random emission of an electron. The task of the PK subject is to try to force the lights round the circle, in a specified direction. That so many have succeeded so well is amazing when one realizes that PK must influence the path of one electron so accurately that it stops the mechanism, which is oscillating at a million times each second, at the precise point which will allow the lamp at the desired position to light up.

Fringe medicine

Many methods of treating the sick do not fit comfortably into any of the systems of modern medicine. Whether or not we class them as 'paranormal' really depends on where we place the dividing line between normal events, which can be readily explained by current medical knowledge, and those which clearly operate by some as yet unknown powers of the mind.

Before considering some of these unusual forms of medical treatment, it is as well to remind ourselves of some of the more baffling examples of the mind's power over the body, which are accepted by orthodox medical science. Probably the most extreme example of this is the so-called 'voodoo death', when as a result of a real or imagined curse, a person wills himself to death.

On a less dramatic level, we have all at some time experienced psychosomatic disorders; headaches, stomach aches, sickness and a whole range of lesser problems which follow a mental or emotional upset.

If the body can produce disorders in itself, under the influence of the mind, then it follows that the mind can effect a cure of the disorders, by cancelling or countermanding its previous instructions to the nervous system. This is a very important principle which must be kept in mind when considering any form of fringe medicine. It is even made use of by orthodox medicine, when doctors prescribe medically inactive placebo medicines which sometimes effect dramatic cures.

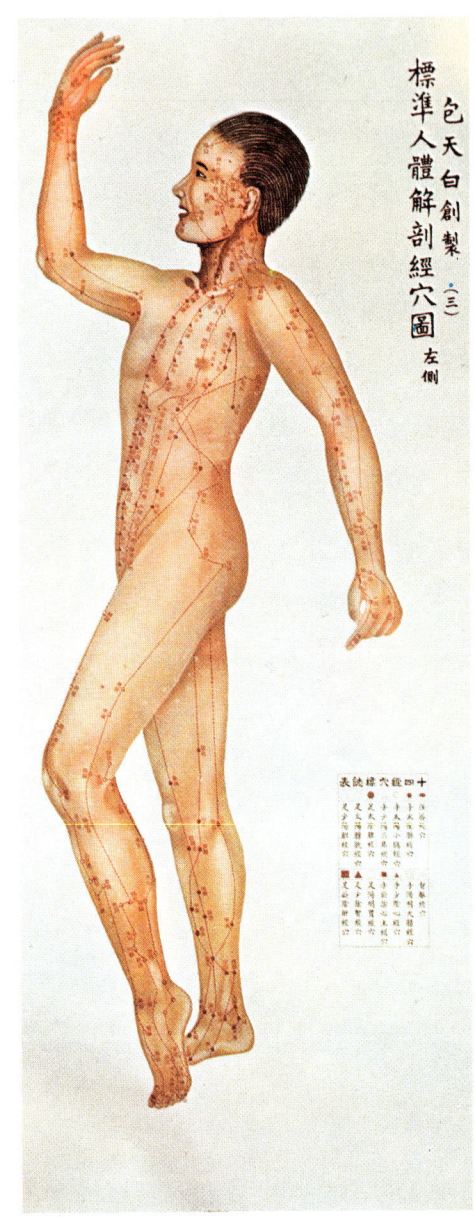

▶ The ancient Chinese art of acupuncture is enjoying a resurgence in China and the rest of the world. This chart shows the many points at which needles can be inserted.

Acupuncture

The ancient Chinese system of medicine called acupuncture is one example of a form of treatment which falls uneasily between orthodox medical method and fringe medicine. For more than 2,000 years Chinese medicine has evolved in isolation from western ideas, and has produced a complicated system of diets, exercises and herbal remedies, of which acupuncture forms only a part. Traditionally, the Chinese paid their doctors only so long as they remained healthy; if they fell sick, payment was withheld.

Acupuncture is based upon the belief that an intangible 'life force' called *ch'i* flows through the body, along a series of 12 main channels or meridians. Along these channels lie 700 or more points at which the flow of *ch'i* can be influenced by the acupuncturist's needles. According to the Chinese theory, sickness results when the flow of *ch'i* along the meridians becomes unbalanced.

Acupuncture needles are inserted in the skin and underlying tissues of the patient at points seemingly unrelated to the area in which pain or disease occurs. When acupuncture is used to induce anaesthesia, for example, before an operation, needles may be inserted in the forearm while the neck is the site of the operation. When operating on the abdomen, needles may be placed in the lobe of the ear. Once in place the needles are usually twirled regularly by the acupuncturist, or in more recently developed techniques, an electric current may be passed down them from wires connected to a battery.

Even the most enthusiastic medical users of acupuncture agree that there is no anatomical justification for their theories. The meridians do not appear to exist, and so far, it has not been possible to demonstrate any structure at the acupuncture points which might give rise to physical changes elsewhere in the body when they are stimulated with the needles. Equally certainly, acupuncture does produce some very interesting physical changes in the body, and some of the main acupuncture points correspond to areas showing a strong response to Kirlian photography.

The use of acupuncture alone as a treatment for disease has not been well accepted in western countries, and even in China is not now widely used. But its use in treating pain, whether it is pain resulting from a disease like arthritis, or pain associated with an operation, seems to offer real benefits. Western doctors have watched oper-

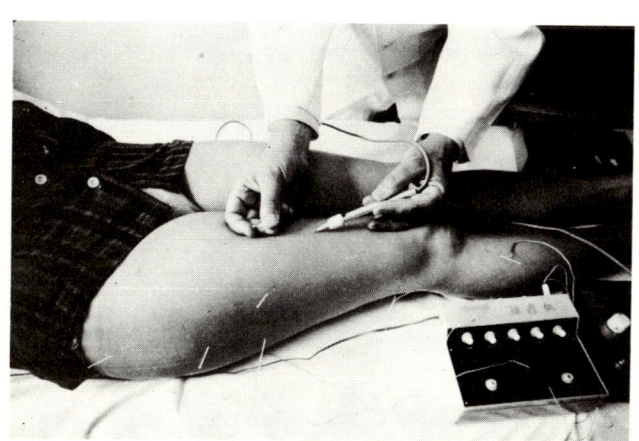

◀ In the modern form of acupuncture, electric currents are passed down the needles to stimulate the nerves, or at least, that is the current medical thinking behind the practice. It is thought that in this way, the passage of nervous signals carrying the sensation of pain can be blocked off from the brain, and a state of local anaesthesia is achieved.

▲ In a homoeopathic dispensary, herbal remedies are diluted with water, then diluted again and again until they contain almost none of the original medicinal substance.

ations carried out under acupuncture anaesthesia in which fully conscious patients have had brain operations, portions of diseased lung removed, or tumours removed, while the patients were able to chat with the surgeons, and even to eat and drink during the operation.

There are some medically 'respectable' theories to account for the control of pain by the acupuncturist's needle. It is thought that the twirling of the needle or the current passed along it may somehow produce interference with the normal passage of nerve impulses which convey the sense of pain to the brain.

Homoeopathy

Similarly placed in a limbo just outside orthodox medicine is the latter-day development of herbal medicine called homoeopathy. This system evolved from an ancient magical belief that 'like cures like'. The principle of homoeopathy is that it is first necessary to find a naturally occurring substance which, when taken in large enough doses, will produce symptoms resembling the disease affecting the patient. According to homoeopathic theory, a very low dose of this substance will then have the effect of *relieving* the symptom in the patient. The theory is then taken to greater lengths, for it is believed that the more any homoeopathic remedy is diluted, the more powerful will be its curative effects. In some cases, this is carried so far that the original preparation is diluted by 100 million parts of water, and even to the extent that mathematical calculation demonstrates that *none* of the molecules from the original mixture still remain.

Because no one has yet come up with a plausible theory on how homoeopathy could work, it has remained on the fringe of current medical science. However, in Britain at least, homoeopathic doctors can practise in the National Health service, and it is quite widely known that the Queen has a consultant homoeopathic physician.

Quite closely related to homoeopathy is the system of healing invented by a Dr Bach in the 1920s, which uses the essence of various types of flowers as curative agents. This technique is currently enjoying a resurgence in Britain and the USA, although in the few scientific tests made on the preparations, analysts have not been able to distinguish them from pure water.

Psychic surgery

Probably the most dramatic manifestation of fringe medicine is the technique known as psychic surgery. There is not, and probably never will be, any 'logical' explanation for the phenomena which apparently occur. It must be either a new and extremely powerful paranormal phenomenon, or a singularly heartless fraud practised on sick people.

The first psychic surgeon to attract popular interest was the Brazilian healer nicknamed 'Arigo'. From 1950 until his death in 1971, Arigo operated on literally thousands of people, using ordinary pocket knives, table knives, razors, or anything else which came to hand. In front of witnesses (many of them visiting physicians from the USA) Arigo apparently slashed open people with these crude tools, and removed huge tumours, then closed the wounds merely by pressing the edges together. No cases of infection were ever recorded after these violent operations, even though absolutely no antiseptic precautions were taken. Photographs of some of his operations are quite disconcerting, some showing patients with large knives pushed up under their eyes or eyelids, apparently without causing any pain.

A less spectacular sideline of Arigo's was instant diagnosis without actually examining the patient, after which he would write out an obscure prescription which reportedly worked very effectively. Not surprisingly, the Brazilian medical authorities bitterly resented Arigo's activities, and persecuted him relentlessly until his death. Meanwhile, however, dozens more psychic surgeons had come to light on the opposite side of the globe, in the Philippines.

Like Arigo, the Filipino surgeons are guided by spirits during their operations. Unlike him, however, they do not use knives to open the flesh of their patients, but cause the flesh to part by psychic means. Or so it appears, although many researchers and investigators believe them to be fraudulent. They seem to push their fingers deep into the bodies of their patients, and remove large masses of tissue with their bare hands. It is possible, of course, that they are merely doubling back their fingers, and that the material they remove has simply been concealed from view beforehand. The blood which appears has been analyzed; sometimes it is human, sometimes animal blood. In one curious instance a tumour removed from a child was given to an investigator for analysis. Somewhat to his surprise it *was* a tumour, but of a type only occurring in breast cancer, and certainly not to be found in children.

Faith healing

Psychic surgery is perhaps an extreme example of faith healing; the laying on of hands which has been so widely used for at

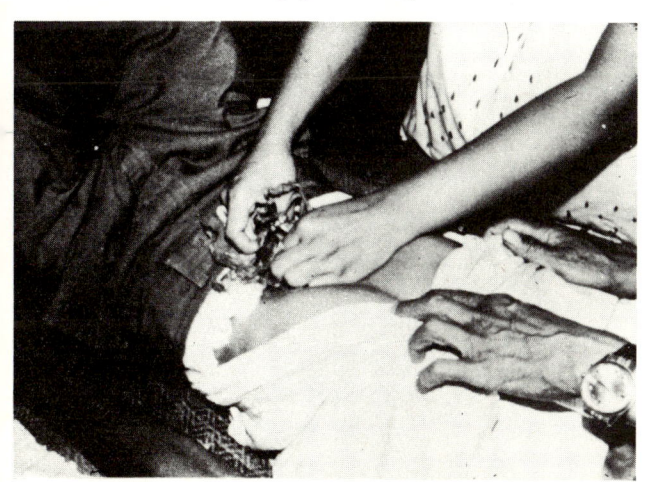

◀ In the Philippines, spiritualist surgeons apparently operate on patients with their bare hands, removing tumours and closing up the wounds without leaving a trace of a scar. It is difficult to decide if they really open the flesh as they claim, or are charlatans relying on clever trickery. Many sick people travel across the world to be treated by them.

least 2,000 years. In many cases, physical contact is not necessary, however, and prayer is the common denominator found in all forms of faith healing. The miracles of the Catholic Church, such as those taking place fairly frequently at Lourdes, have in recent years been studied painstakingly by qualified medical researchers before being accepted as of divine origin. Some of these are completely inexplicable by the tenets of modern medical science, although this does not preclude the rare spontaneous cures which sometimes occur, particularly with diseases like cancer, when the body suddenly seems to heal itself.

There is also objective evidence of lasting beneficial results obtained by faith healers. A German healer was studied in 1955, in a series of 538 patients. Most were chronic sufferers, who had been having orthodox treatment for five years or more. After their healing treatment, medical assessors found that nine per cent had actual physical improvement, and 61 per cent felt better or had temporary physical improvements in their condition. On the other hand, half the patients whose conditions had actually deteriorated said that they felt better, showing the effect of suggestion and faith.

Estebany

Suggestion may be the cause of many apparent cures, but in experiments on the healing of animals, this could not be the explanation for the improved rate of healing which was found. The experiments were carried out on mice, which were given small skin wounds. The medium, a Hungarian called Estebany, held the injured mice in his cupped hands for 20 minutes at a time, twice each day. As a comparison, students handled another group of mice for the same length of time, and a third identical group were not handled at all. The group of mice handled by Estebany healed significantly faster than the other groups.

Even stranger results were obtained when

◀ Harry Edwards was the most famous of British Spiritual healers, and treated many thousands of patients in his clinic. Healing produces good results in patients suffering from pain, and from diseases which can be influenced by the mind, such as asthma, skin rashes, and a variety of internal disorders. Like hypnosis, healing can have a powerful effect on people who are suggestible, although the beneficial results are not always sustained.

Estebany took part in experiments on plants. Barley seeds were soaked in salty water to weaken them, then baked gently for long enough to injure them still further. When the seeds were planted, it was found that those which had been soaked in salt water from a bottle which had been handled by Estebany grew much more vigorously than the other plants. It was thought that if a healer could stimulate growth, then perhaps some people might have the reverse effect. The experiment was repeated with a psychologically normal person and two patients suffering from severe depression handling the bottles. Seeds soaked in water from the bottles held by the depressed patients grew poorly, compared to the other seeds.

Other experimenters found that Estebany could increase the speed of a biochemical reaction taking place in a test tube, and by the simple laying on of hands, increased the red blood cell count of hospitalized patients.

There is some evidence for an unusual type of energy being produced by healers, such as the flares of light which have been recorded in experiments with Kirlian photography. Olga Worrall, an American healer, has been able to produce strange wave-like patterns in a device known as a cloud chamber, which is used in high-energy physics to detect intangible particles like cosmic rays and neutrons emitted from radioactive substances. If confirmed, these experiments would permit an alternative explanation to that of 'suggestion'.

Radiesthesia

Some more 'sophisticated' devices seem to rely for their efficacy on looking very impressive, but beneath the complex consoles covered in dials and knobs, there is usually nothing remotely resembling a workable circuit. Even if there were effective components in these 'black boxes' used for radiesthesia, it is difficult to see how they could

▲ Radiesthesia is a method of healing which uses an impressive machine for both diagnosing and treating patients. This is often combined with the use of the dowser's pendulum, as a sensitive detection device. Using this equipment, radiesthesists diagnose and treat patients whom they may never meet, using only a drop of blood on a piece of paper as their contact with the patient.

diagnose disease from a drop of blood placed in the machine, as they are claimed to, still less to actually treat the disease in a patient who may be far away. In some of these radionic machines, the operator obtains a reading by rubbing his fingers gently back and forth on a plate built into the machine, while manipulating the dials. When the correct reading is reached, the operator is said to feel a 'stickiness' on the plate. There are a number of variants of these medical machines, and in the USA in particular, their users have been fiercely attacked by the F&DA, the body which regulates drugs and medicines. This was carried to such a pitch that Wilhelm Reich, a respected psychiatrist with individualistic views on treatment of disease with a device he called the 'orgone accumulator', was actually imprisoned after the F&DA ordered all his devices and books to be destroyed.

69

Dowsing

The ancient art of dowsing is the most practical of all forms of ESP. It also produces the most consistent results. Professional dowsers are employed by farmers, water authorities, and civil engineers in order to locate sources of underground water. In Vietnam and elsewhere, dowsers were used to find mines and hidden dugouts, and occasionally, police forces have called on the services of a dowser to help them locate a body. The techniques of dowsing are basically very simple and the dowser, unlike many other exponents of paranormal ability, does not have to cultivate any special mental state when exercising his powers.

The forked twig (1) is the simplest tool for dowsing, but its use demands a certain amount of practice, particularly in grasping the twig correctly. It is important to select twigs which can be cut so that the two branches are of equal thickness (2). Plastic strip like that used for drawing instruments can also be made into a dowsing device. Use strips (3) about 20 mm ($\frac{3}{4}$ in) wide, and join the ends by taping them or by riveting with an eyelet punch, of the type which can be bought in a stationers. Simplest of all to use are the rods made from a pair of wire coat hangers (4). Wooden or plastic grips can be added to make them more sensitive (5). Other materials can be used for the rods, such as welding rod or heavy gauge piano wire. Pendulums can be improvised from any small weight, but some people like to use hollow types, in which specimen samples can be placed (6).

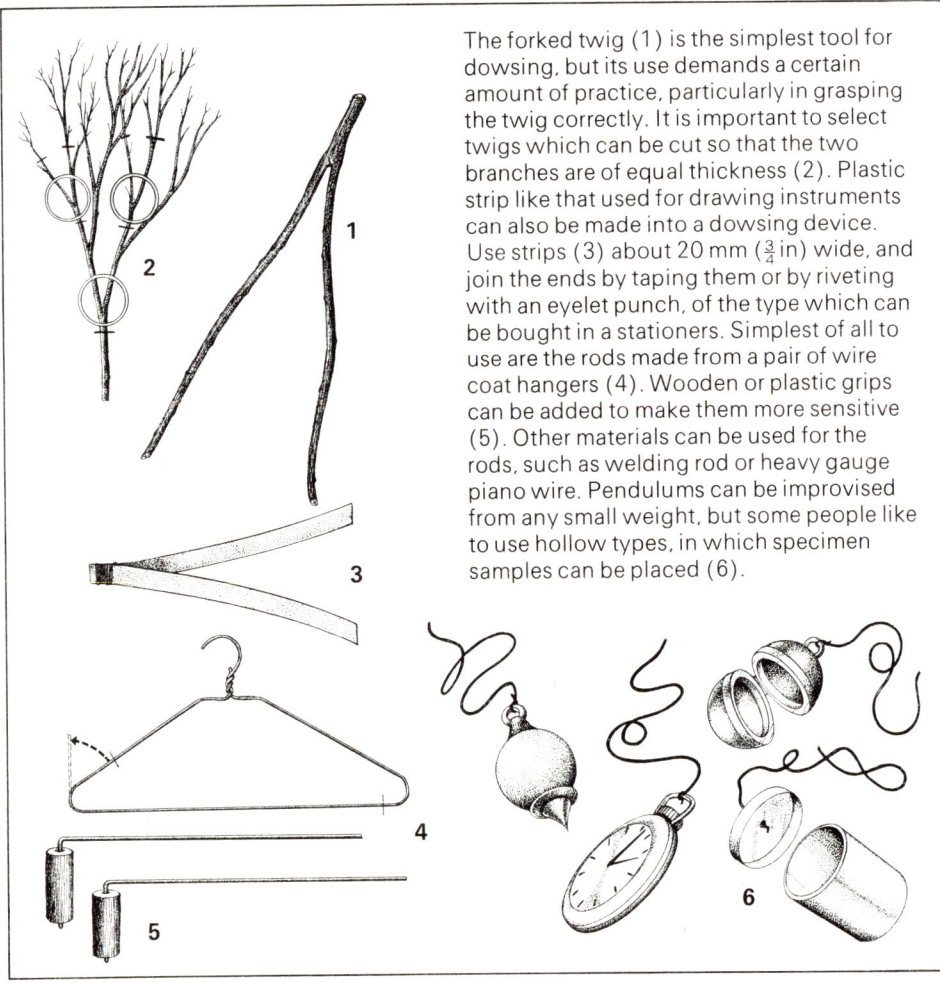

The dowsing twig

The use of a forked twig is the classic dowsing technique, which has persisted unchanged for hundreds of years. The basic requirement is a freshly-cut forked twig, made of a strong yet resilient wood, with both arms of the fork of about the same thickness. The branch is cut so that there are two long forks, while the thicker main branch is cut off short. The size is immaterial. The dowsing twig will work equally well if it is anywhere between 70mm (3 in) and a metre in length, although total length of about 45 cm (18 in) is probably most suitable. The type of wood you select is very important. Not many trees produce twigs which have equal sized branches, but you must persevere until you find one. Hazel is the traditional material, but branches of weeping willow make particularly suitable twigs, as also does the poplar.

The reason for selecting such springy material becomes clear when you grip the twig. You can hold the forks in your clenched fists, or trapped between thumbs and clenched knuckles. Having gripped them firmly, you must then bend your wrists inwards so that the arms of the twig flex. As you do this, the point of the twig will either rise or fall, and you will have to adjust your grip slightly in order to make it come to rest in a level position. Keep your elbows well out from your side, and practise walking to and fro, keeping the twig fairly level. This is the basic technique for dowsing.

The Dowsing rods

Simple L-shaped rods are a relatively new dowsing tool, and are simplest of all to use. They are held lightly in the hands, and the wrists are rotated slightly until both rods swing forward and come to rest parallel with the ground and with each other. Once more, you will need to practise walking about with them in order to keep them fairly steady.

More sophisticated rods can be made, or purchased complete. They will swing more freely if hand-grips are fitted. These can be made from pieces of dowelling with a small hole drilled part-way down the middle. Small plastic containers like those used for mascara and other cosmetics will also suit. You may like to experiment with different sizes of rods. Larger rods are less sensitive, but are also less likely to be blown about by the wind.

The pendulum

The third dowsing technique, which is also very old, is a simple pendulum; a small weight swinging on the end of a string. To make a pendulum, you must first select a suitable weight Professional pendulums can be purchased, but yours can be made from any material you like. The only

▲ Lloyd George and his wife demonstrate two basic methods of gripping dowsing rods.

special thing about a pendulum is that it must be symmetrical, so that the string can be attached to the exact centre, as it will otherwise not swing smoothly. The bob-weights used on builders' plumblines are ideal, and you may be lucky enough to find one in a hardware shop. You may be able to find a plastic knob intended for a cupboard handle which is of a suitable size—about 20 mm ($\frac{3}{4}$ in) diameter.

As with the other types of dowsing tools, you must practise the way to hold your pendulum while walking about. Don't try and

▼ Hold your pendulum between finger and thumb (1), and allow it to swing gently (2). When near your target it should circle (3).

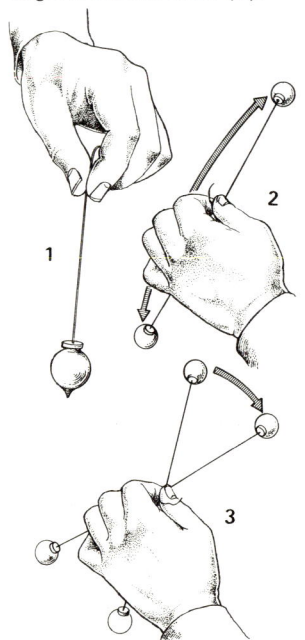

brace your arm against your side; just hold it partly outstretched and relaxed, and concentrate on letting the pendulum swing gently to and fro.

Dowsing techniques

Whether you are using the twig, rods, or a pendulum, your dowsing tool is going to act as a very simple yet sensitive mechanical amplifier of the tiny muscular movements in your wrists and arms when you are near your target. It seems quite clear that there is no paranormal link with your dowsing tool; its movements simply exaggerate those of your own body. A few very accomplished dowsers can even work with their bare hands.

So how do you use your dowsing tool? In its simplest form, dowsing involves walking slowly across ground under which it is thought water may flow. The dowsing tool should indicate the presence of water. If you use the twig, it will dip as you near the flowing water. Rods swing together until they cross over, roughly parallel to the direction of flow of the water. Your pendulum will change its motion from a regular to-and-fro swing to a circular swinging. To some extent, this movement in the dowsing tool is determined by your own expectations. If you think the twig should *rise* when you are near water, then this is what will actually happen. You must decide in advance on the response which will tell you that water is there. When you do get a

positive response, there will be no doubt that *something* is happening. A twig circles down so strongly that it is very difficult to stop its movement—it may even break. Similarly, with the other devices, you will not be conscious of influencing their movement.

Once you have a response (and probably 50 per cent of amateurs *can* obtain a response), try and confirm whether or not water is likely to be present. Along the edge of a ditch, you may find field drains from which water is trickling, and the course of the drains can be plotted. In a garden, you may find that manhole covers indicate the course of water mains or sewers. Except by the drastic course of digging a well it is difficult to prove that you are really successful, however.

You can try and determine the depth of the water you detect by the simple dowsers' expedient called the Bishop's Rule. Briefly, this states that you will get a response at a distance from your target which is equivalent to its depth below ground. So as you approach a pipe two metres below ground, you should notice a weak response when you are two metres away, a strong response as you move over the pipe, and a further weak response as you pass out of range, two metres on the further side of the pipe. This requires much practice, and you will have to be competent at first distinguishing the main response from your target.

Dowsing need not be confined to locating water. Some people can find minerals, coins, and a wide range of other items. But whatever you are seeking, you must have a firm image of your target in your mind; don't just dowse at random, or you will only pick up random responses.

Dowsing from afar

With practice, you can refine your technique so that you can dowse from a distance, without having to actually walk across your hidden target. Extend your arm or use a long wooden pointer, and turn so that your 'pointer' scans over the area you are investigating. As you turn, watch the pendulum held in your other hand, and stop when it begins to gyrate. Using sticks, mark the direction you have indicated, then move a little way off and repeat the process. Where the two lines you have marked intersect, you should find your target. The same process can be repeated on a map, using a pencil as a pointer, although this type of dowsing requires a lot of practice.

Another type of pendulum dowsing which can provide you with more information on your target is the system perfected by the late Tom Lethbridge, using a long pendulum. Lethbridge devised a series of pendulum rates, or string lengths, each corresponding to a different target. A pendulum length of 56cm (22in), for example, is used for seeking silver or lead; 71cm (28in) for tin; 73cm (29in) for gold. Lethbridge's books contain detailed tables of pendulum rates, but it is probably best to establish your own by experimentation, as you will find that your own reading may be quite different from those established by other dowsers.

Similar results are also obtained by using a hollow pendulum weight, inside which is fitted a sample of the substance being sought. If you prefer to use rods, you can hold a sample in one hand, touching the rod. It is doubtful if these samples have any more than a symbolic function, serving to remind the dowser more forcibly of the target he is seeking.

▼ As you walk towards your target (1), your dowsing instrument should give a firm indication. The forked twig will probably dip (2), the pendulum should circle (3), and the rods cross over (4).

Telepathy and clairvoyance

If you are lucky enough to have a marked talent for telepathy or clairvoyance, you probably already know of it, and use your talent to some extent in day-to-day life. The power of ESP varies enormously, however, and probably most people have *some* degree of paranormal ability, although this is usually unused, at least until it has been recognized. Once you have identified any ESP abilities you may have, you can begin to train yourself to use them more effectively. But however convinced you are of the abilities you seem to possess, you must accept that other people will not be convinced so easily.

Techniques for studying telepathy and clairvoyance are well-established, and the easiest for the amateur to use are those based on the Zener cards developed by J. B. Rhine. You can buy packs of 25 Zener cards from some of the specialist bookshops specializing in the paranormal and the occult, or from the Society for Psychical Research. If you prefer to make your own, they can be made from simple and easily available materials. The basic five symbols used (circle, square, triangle, cross, and wavy lines) must be drawn on cards, so that you have five cards bearing each symbol. It is important that the drawing does not show through, so if you draw them directly on the surface, use very thick card.

Boredom can adversely affect the results of ESP tests, due to the unemotional symbols used. You may like to make up a set of cards bearing symbols which have strong emotional meaning for you, such as members of your family, your home, and so on.

Recording scores
The other thing you will need

▲ You can purchase ready-made Zener cards for ESP experiments, or make up your own using these simple symbols. Always be scrupulously accurate in recording your scores, as even a small error can make random results look like ESP.

is a chart to record your scores. This is simply a card bearing columns, each divided into 25 boxes.

The easiest type of ESP to test is clairvoyance. Shuffle your cards thoroughly, and place them face-down on the table. Now write down what you believe to be the symbol on the top card, remove it without turning it over, and write what you believe to be the symbol on the next, and so on, right through the pack. Now turn the pack over, and check your results, filling in the actual symbols next to your guesses. As a variant, try turning each card over after each guess.

Telepathy is tested in much the same way, using an assistant as the 'sender'. In this case, the sender has the pack of shuffled cards, and turns them over singly, calling 'now' as he turns each. You must obviously be out of actual sight of the cards, and record your guesses each time your partner indicates that a card has been turned over.

In either telepathy or clairvoyance, you would expect to guess five correct cards out of each run through the set. Keep repeating the test, and when you feel tired, check your average score by dividing the total score by the number of complete runs you have made. If you are consistently scoring above five, there is a possibility that ESP has occurred, although it would take much more sophisticated tests to prove this conclusively.

Psycho-kinesis

Most forms of ESP seem to depend on an extension of our normal capacity for intuition. We seldom know definitely when it is working, and it is quite difficult to demonstrate even when working effectively. So it is only to be expected that psychokinesis, or moving objects by mental power, will be more difficult to accomplish, and correspondingly more dramatic when it does occur.

When you first try to use the power of your mind to move a physical object, it is probable that your power, if any, is only weak (an obvious exception would be people associated with poltergeist phenomena, who seem to have a powerful, though poorly controlled, PK ability). It seems sensible to try and develop PK by attempting to move the lightest possible objects before trying more ambitious feats.

Smoke is just about the lightest material with which you can test your PK ability. If you blow out a mouthful of cigarette smoke, very gently, through a long straw which extends into a tall glass, you can produce a 'puddle' of smoke in the bottom of the glass which will persist for several minutes, particularly if the glass is covered with a saucer to eliminate draughts. Now concentrate on the smoke. Envisage it bubbling up in the middle, or collecting at one side of the glass. You may be lucky enough to produce distinct movement in this lightest of all targets.

Moving pendulum

If you prefer to try your skills on something a little more tangible, you can make up a very light pendulum. First take a crumb of expanded polystyrene (the material used as an insulating and packing material), selecting a piece about the size of a pea. Stretch a hair between your fingers, and press it against the crumb of plastic. It should cut its way in, while the plastic grips it firmly. Attach the other end of the hair to the bottom of a tumbler, as shown in the diagram, using a piece of adhesive tape, 'Plasticine', or a spot of glue. When you invert the tumbler, you will have a tiny sensitive pendulum, protected beneath the glass.

Now concentrate on the pendulum, and try to make it swing. Quite probably you will succeed. Did you have your elbows on the table? Place the glass on the floor and try again. Still moving? Now place it on a concrete floor, where no vibrations at

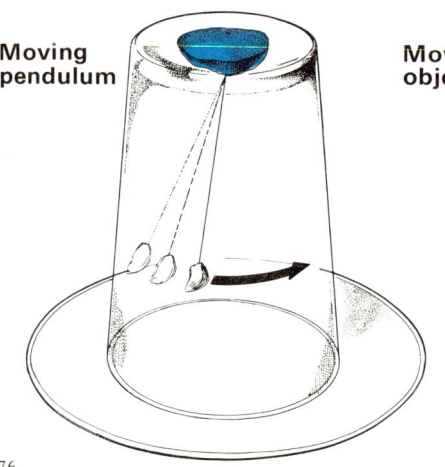

Moving pendulum

Moving floating object

all can reach it. If you can still move the pendulum, you may very well have some PK ability (although static electricity in your body can also make it move!).

Unfortunately, the more sensitive you make your target, the easier it becomes for such unsuspected outside influences to affect your results.

Moving floating object

You can make another sensitive PK detector with the aid of a glass of water. If you pour water very carefully into a clean glass, you can actually get the water surface to stand clear above the rim of the glass, retained by the elastic film called the meniscus. If you float your PK target on this invisible film, it can revolve freely on the water surface under the influence of PK. You have a considerable choice of targets. If you want to try moving magnetic material, place an ordinary needle gently on the film, using a pair of tweezers. It will float, supported by the meniscus. You can also try non-magnetic metals like aluminium, by using a scrap of cooking foil as a target. Wooden matchsticks and plastic toothpicks are equally satisfactory target objects.

Whatever you use, you must concentrate on causing the target to rotate on the water surface. You have already seen some complicating factors in the experiment with the pendulum, so presumably you are not moving the table with your elbows. But is your face close enough to the glass for its warmth to cause tiny air currents to circulate and cause the target to move? Are you sure that breath from your mouth or nose is not causing a draught? Invert a large glass or jug over the whole thing to eliminate these possibilities, and keep trying.

Dice throwing

Most people think of dice as the obvious PK target, although they have the disadvantage that clairvoyance would be needed to know where the target face would be as the dice rolled, and they are comparatively heavy objects to move. Shaking a dice in a plastic cup means that you eliminate any bias in rolling it. You must decide in advance on the number you wish to throw, and concentrate on that number. You have a one-in-six chance of rolling that number by chance. Repeated tests increase the likelihood that any success you achieve is actually PK. However, the dice is probably slightly biased, particularly if the spots are drilled into the surface. This would make the 'six' lightest, and it will come up more often than chance would predict. You can overcome this problem by trying to roll numbers selected at random. Open a telephone directory at any page, and write down the numbers one to six as they appear in the final digit in the column of telephone numbers. These will be in as near random sequence as possible for our purposes. Now try to roll the numbers you have listed.

As with tests on telepathy and clairvoyance, you should repeat the tests as many times as possible, then divide the number of tests into your total score to see if you are consistently scoring better than the success rate of one in six which chance would predict. You will need sophisticated statistics to decide if your results are truly significant, but this is outside the scope of this book.

77

Getting the message

There are a number of well-established techniques for communicating with the spirits, if you subscribe to belief in an afterlife, or for obtaining information from your subconscious mind, should you prefer a 'rational' explanation. Some of these techniques have been severely criticized, and many people believe that 'meddling with the unknown' is a sure recipe for disaster. If you are of a particularly sensitive disposition, or think you are neurotic in any way, *don't* try and communicate with the unknown. Whether you contact spirits or the darker recesses of your own mind, you will quite probably receive some unpalatable or disturbing messages.

One of the most reliable methods of obtaining messages by apparently paranormal means is automatic writing. Most people find it helpful to have a simple mechanical device to help them, such as the planchette (see below). Its use is very simple, although as with other forms of communication, you will have to cultivate the correct frame of mind before getting any reliable results.

Place your hand on the planchette, keeping your elbow raised from the surface of the table, and your arm as relaxed as possible. Now relax, and consider the type of message you hope to receive. If you are seeking the answer to a problem, consider all the facets and aspects of that problem. Should you wish to contact the spirits, fix an image of the person you wish to communicate with firmly in your mind. Then stop trying, and start a train of thought which takes you off on a different track. As an aid to relaxation, you may like to have music playing softly, and the lights lowered. If you are lucky, and if you have any talent for mediumship, you may suddenly realize that your hand has been moving the planchette across the paper for some time, and amid the scrawl produced, there may be recognizable words.

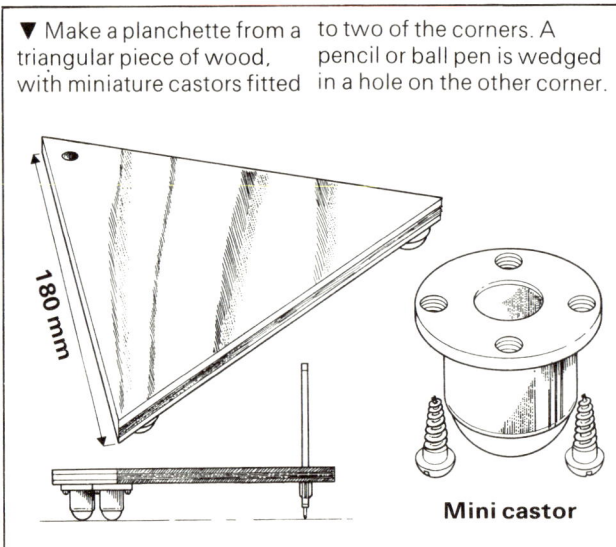

▼ Make a planchette from a triangular piece of wood, with miniature castors fitted to two of the corners. A pencil or ball pen is wedged in a hole on the other corner.

Mini castor

▲ In use, the hand is placed lightly on the planchette, which can move freely across a piece of paper.

▲ Sitters place their fingers on the ouija pointer, which moves to spell out its message.

The ouija board
Most people have played the old 'mirror and glass' party game, which is a crude version of the ouija board. The technique is simple; around the edge of a polished table (or a mirror placed face up on a table can be used) are placed scraps of paper on which are written the letters of the alphabet, and the words 'yes' and 'no'. An inverted glass is stood on the mirror, and on the base of this, all those participating in the seance place their forefingers. One person asks aloud if the spirits have a message; usually the answer is 'yes', and the glass moves about the mirror, spelling out the name of the person for whom the message is intended, and producing the message itself.

Sometimes the messages produced are trite, but on other occasions, they can be so revealing as to cause considerable embarassment to the sitters. It is only too easy to 'cheat' by pushing the glass, and probably the subconscious mind cheats in the same way in producing these unwelcome messages.

Scrying
Some methods of divination or communication probably require a certain degree of self-hypnosis to be successful. In automatic writing, for example, the detached and relaxed mood necessary for successful communication is referred to by psychologists as an 'altered state of consciousness'. In scrying, or divination by means of a mirror, crystal ball, or other aid, it is necessary to induce a mental state where one begins to hallucinate, although this is not as alarming as it sounds.

The easiest way to try this is to make a scrying mirror. This can be made from an old clock glass; the curved window covering a clock face. Paint it black on the *hollow* side, then attach it to a board with flexible mastic or putty. When you try scrying, sit with your mirror in a darkened room, and make sure you are unlikely to be interrupted. Look into your mirror; not at the images you see reflected, but deep into it, letting your eyes go slightly out of focus. Try to visualize the person you are trying to reach, or the place you wish to see. Don't try too hard, but if nothing happens for a while, try to keep the image in your mind for as long as possible. Unlike most of the other phenomena we have discussed, scrying tends to work best when you are tired. You may start to see images forming, first just as a quick flash, too fast to be sure you have seen anything. Accomplished scryers see continuous images like a tiny television screen. Are they really seeing with the eyes, or with the mind's eye? It really doesn't matter. If you are a talented medium, you can probably develop the facility of communication without any aids at all.

Who's kidding who?

It is very easy to convince oneself that a paranormal event has occurred, and easier still to persuade gullible people. Unfortunately, parapsychology has been bedevilled with fraud and trickery, which has often obscured the less spectacular occurrences which seem to be genuinely paranormal. Some simple tricks which look like ESP to the uninitiated actually demand a considerable knowledge of human behaviour if they are to work effectively. They can be amusing party tricks, and their success should make you more critical of the performances of some dubious 'psychics', and respectful of the talents of stage magicians who do not claim any paranormal powers.

◀ This is a carefully posed version of the Indian Rope Trick. The original probably depends on suggestion and mass hypnosis.

There are numerous books available which explain how to carry out a number of 'magic' tricks which look very much like ESP. Some stage magicians are so impressive that their admirers often insist that they have paranormal abilities, in spite of all their denials to the contrary. The most ludicrous example of this sort of attitude was the belief, which is still current, that the famous illusionist Harry Houdini was actually an accomplished psychic. This belief was current in spite of the fact that Houdini spent a large part of his life exposing fraudulent mediums, and never found one he could accept as genuine.

Talking pendulums

About 75 years ago, some fraudulent mediums used a simple yet impressive demonstration with pendulums as proof of their powers. You can repeat this very easily, taking advantage of some of the drawbacks we have seen with genuine tests

◀ Using the 'Talking Pendulums', messages can be spelled out, and questions answered. The movement of the pendulums is controlled by the sitters, although they are unaware of this.

of ESP ability. First you must obtain the cooperation of several other people. Ask them for signet rings, wedding rigs, or any other small object of personal value. These must each be tied on a length of thread. As the diagram shows, the threads are then tied to a ruler, which is in turn balanced over the necks of two bottles. This is arranged so that the rings are suspended inside wine glasses or tumblers, but not touching the sides. Your 'talking' pendulums are now ready.

With your apparatus set up on a small table, ask your helpers to place their hands flat on the table. You need take no direct part in the proceedings. Explain that you will all attempt to move one of the rings by PK, or by the help of spirits, if you prefer. Draw the attention of your helpers to the ring which is to be moved, or let them select one. Now you must all concentrate. Within a few seconds, it will begin to swing, faster and faster, until it strikes the side of the glass. Now choose another; that too will swing until it jingles against the glass, while the first comes to a halt.

How does it work? Very simply, the sitters are causing tiny vibrations from their hands to shake the table slightly. These vibrations stir the pendulums and when the sitters subconsciously note the desired pendulum move, they vary the rate of the tiny movements, quite unknowingly. In this way, they increase the rate of swing, until the pendulum eventually strikes the side of the glass.

Why does the other pendulum or pendulums not swing at the same rate? The speed at which a pendulum swings is governed by the length of the string, and in this case, all the pendulums are of slightly different lengths. So the amount of vibration which causes our target pendulum to swing regularly will only cause a slight wobbling in the others.

As soon as the sitters' attention is directed to one of the others, the rate of vibration alters, to set it swinging, and the first pendulum comes slowly to rest.

The same effect can often be demonstrated in seances using the ouija board, in which no trickery is intended. When the sitters see the pointer moving towards letters which might complete a word already partially spelled out, their anticipation is enough to vary their finger pressure on the pointer, and ensure that the expected word is in fact spelled out.

The simple expedient of covering the board with a piece of opaque card, supported high enough above the surface to allow the sitters' hands to move freely beneath it, demonstrates that it is the sitters' ability to see the movement of the pointer which controls its messages. When the board is covered in this way and an observer sitting to one side records the 'message', it will generally 'write' nothing but complete gibberish.

Hunting the thimble

Most 'pseudo-psychic' events depend for their success on the desire of the participants to obtain results, even though they may be making a conscious effort to be objective. One of the most convincing demonstrations of this attitude is the 'mind-reading' trick, where a 'psychic' finds an object which has been carefully concealed while he was outside the room. With practice, you can probably do this yourself.

For this variant of 'hunt the thimble', it is best, and most impressive, to allow yourself to be blindfolded. After the object has been concealed, you are brought back into the room by a guide. Hold this person's wrist lightly, and move about the room at random. You will find that the normal slight muscular tension in the guide's wrist is less apparent when you move in a certain direction, and by using these small variations, you can locate the part of the room in which the object is hidden by a process of elimination.

There is less mystery about finding the actual hiding place, as it is completely impossible to blindfold someone so that all vision is cut off — even by taping over the eye sockets. By 'peeking' down your nose, you will always be able to see a small and restricted area. This tiny visual assistance, coupled with the continuing aid from involuntary cues given by your guide should enable you to locate the target. Using this technique, a skilled illusionist has been able to find a needle hidden on the far side of town, driving along with one hand on his guide's wrist. You certainly won't be able to duplicate this feat, but you will soon come to recognize the large number of involuntary cues given by anyone taking part in experiments in ESP, or in stage magic. Without these cues, much stage magic would not work.

Pseudolevitation

With the aid of a little concentration and much suggestion, a small group of people can cause a person to rise into the air, supported only by their fingertips, in a way which seems completely beyond our normal strength. Your subject must be sitting on a chair, with feet together, elbows at the sides, and hands clasped in the lap. You will need six assistants, and the trick is more spectacular if these are children. Each of the assistants extends one forefinger, and these are held beneath the knees, elbows and armpits of your subject. Now you must stand in front of your subject, and press down firmly on his head with the flat of your hand, at the same time asking everyone concerned to concentrate hard on making the subject rise into the air. When you think everyone is tense enough, remove your hand suddenly, and shout 'Now' in as impressive a manner as you can. Your subject will rise into the air, supported only by six fingertips.

Preserving pyramid

Occultists have long suspected that there were some mysterious powers associated with the pyramids in Egypt, and in particular, with the Great Pyramid of Cheops. A French visitor to the pyramid, called Bovis, noticed that cats and other small animals that had wandered into the pyramid and died became mummified, and did not putrefy. He experimented with a small model of the pyramid, about a metre square, and succeeded in mummifying a cat placed in a position corresponding to that of the King's burial chamber. This work came to the notice of a Czech engineer, who repeated the experiment, and found that his small pyramids could preserve a wide range of perishable materials. Drbal then made the further discovery that his small pyramid could cause blunted razor blades to become sharp again, after a period of a few days. This only worked when the pyramid was correctly aligned with the earth's magnetic field, and when ordinary blades, rather than the stainless type, were used. Unlikely as this may seem, Drbal managed to obtain a Czech patent for his razor blade sharpener, which can now be bought from suppliers specializing in occult paraphernalia. You can make a small pyramid out of stiff card, using the pattern below, and test these claims for yourself.

The pyramid must be taped or glued together, then placed well away from electrical devices, with the base lines oriented exactly along the magnetic north/south, east/west axes.

Now you can try out the power of your pyramid in preserving food. If you place small pieces of perishable food on the card platform, situated exactly under the apex of the pyramid, according to theory it should gradually dry out without decay. Scale up the whole thing and try it with larger items, if you wish.

The other claimed property of the pyramid is to restore the sharp edge on blunted razor blades. Place the blade on the card platform, with the sharp edges aligned east/west. Within a few days it should be sharp once more. Try it and see!

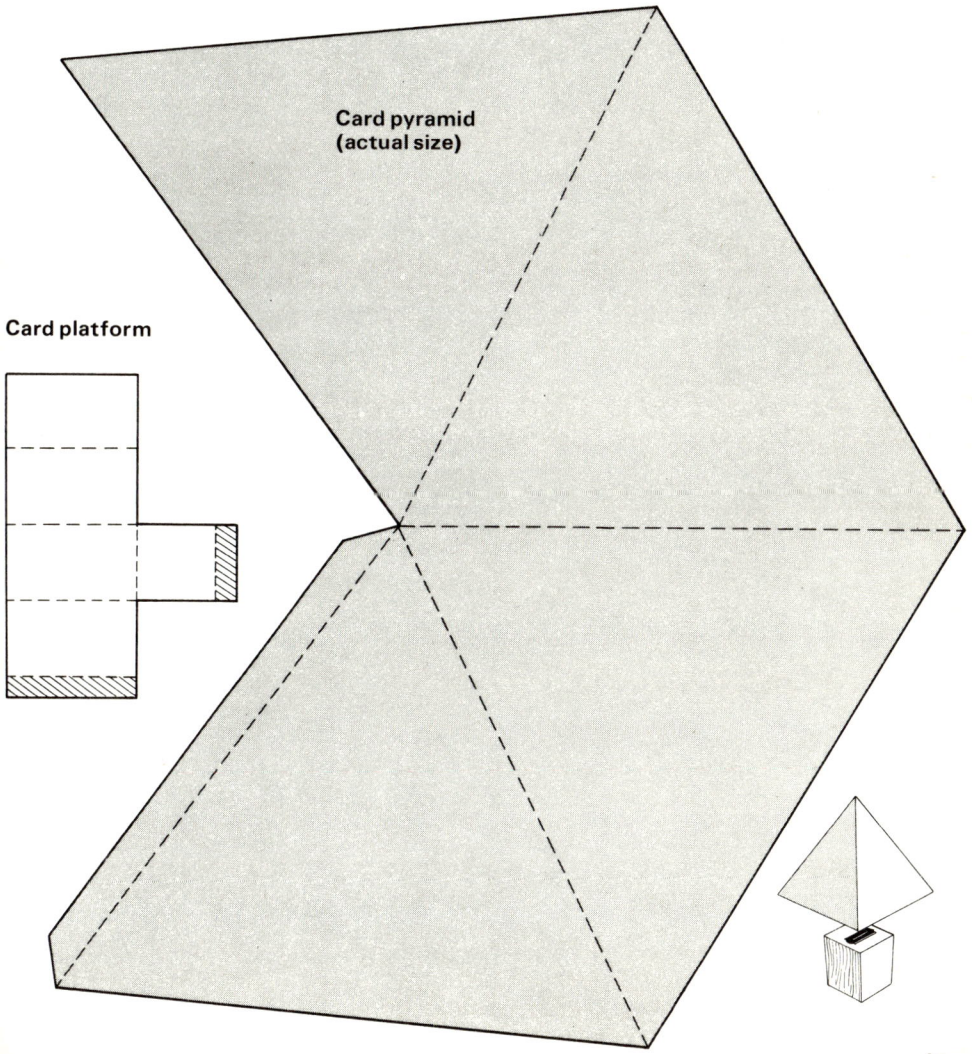

Card pyramid (actual size)

Card platform

Biographies

Early precedents for psychic phenomena are endless, although most are associated with religious beliefs and with magic. Most of the phenomena now accepted as suitable subjects for research can be traced back through time, although the interpretations which were placed on them were vastly different from our own. In pre-Roman Britain, for example, the druid Bladud was said to have caused a rock to fly, bearing him with it, and crashed to his death on the site of the modern St Pauls.

Mother Shipton, born in 1488, gained fame as a prophet, and according to legend, her childhood was plagued with poltergeist phenomena and a whole range of other psychic events. She is said to have predicted the invention of trains and the telegraph.

Friedrich Anton Mesmer was born in Austria in 1734. By 1778, in Paris, he had gained fame as an hypnotic therapist, treating patients by his own concept of 'animal magnetism'. He induced trances in his patients, many of whom had convulsive fits, after which their symptoms often cleared up. Most of his success was probably in patients with psychosomatic illnesses.

Ira and William Davenport were two of the best-known mediums of the 19th century.

They first became known soon after the Fox sisters began to give demonstrations of spirit rapping, and were chiefly noted for their production of astonishing physical effects. While they were tied hand and foot, musical instruments hung near them in a darkened room played without apparent human intervention. In other demonstrations they were tied up in a wooden cabinet, and produced spirit hands at the entrance to the box. They were supreme showmen, and their psychic abilities have never been proved to the satisfaction of later researchers.

The Fox sisters, Margaret and Kate, initiated the interest in spirit phenomena which swept British and American society in the latter part of the 19th century. They first began to produce spirit rappings, and later were associated with almost all of the more dramatic physical manifestations of mediumship. Their later career was bedevilled by accusations of trickery, and even now, it is not clear exactly how much of their repertoire was genuine. Her later confessions of having used fraud were made when Margaret Fox was elderly, unwell, and suffering from alchoholism.

Sir William Crookes, 1832-1919, was one of the most eminent psychic researchers of his time, and as President of the Royal Society, a highly respected physicist. He investigated the medium D. D. Home at length, and was convinced of the validity of his powers. This led to severe criticism of him from fellow scientists, and these attacks increased when his name was linked with that of the medium Florence Cook by the scandal-mongers of the time.

Grigori Rasputin is best known now for his uncanny influence over the Empress Alexandra of Russia, and his apparent powers of healing which saved the life of the Czarevitch Alexis, who suffered from haemophilia. He was a monk who had belonged to a sect called the Khlysty, which indulged in hysterical religious spectacles at which apparent miracles occured. Rasputin had amazing powers of suggestion upon suitably compliant people, and using them, worked his way into the Royal Court, his influence there becoming so strong that he may have been one of the precipitating factors leading to the Russian Revolution.

Eusapia Palladino, born in Italy in 1854, was either one of the most powerful mediums the world has ever seen, or a

consummate actress. Modern psychic researchers are still deeply divided over her abilities, and the consensus of opinion seems to be that she was in fact an accomplished medium, although when her powers were not working well, or if she thought the phenomena being produced were not spectacular enough, she would resort to trickery, and was several times caught in the act. The effects she produced while being investigated by competent researchers included levitation of chairs and tables, and of Eusapia herself. She could also cause small flickering lights to float in the air in the seance room, while tambourines and guitars floated about, playing in mid-air. Eusapia was not especially interested in proving her powers, but cooperated in a large number of studies. Her abilities waned towards the end of her life in 1918, and her later seances were inconclusive.

Harry Houdini, 1874-1926, was the most famous illusionist the world has known. In the latter part of his life, he devoted much of his time to unmasking mediums who used similar illusionist's tricks to produce their effects. Many people believed that Houdini's own performances were carried out by paranormal means. His interest in the psychic world came after his mother's death, when he hoped to contact her through a medium, but soon became disillusioned. Houdini had a standing offer of $10,000 which would be paid to any

medium who could convince him of the genuineness of their phenomena, but the award was never claimed. After his death in a tragic accident, seances began, to see if Houdini himself could escape death and make contact with his friends and family. Only recently they were discontinued; nothing further had been heard from Houdini.

Gerard Croiset, born in 1909, is popularly known as 'the Wizard of Utrecht'. He had clairvoyant abilities from a very early age, and some of these became apparent while he was still a schoolboy, when he told his teacher that he had spent the previous day in the company of a woman who wore a red rose on her dress, and whom the teacher would ultimately marry. This proved to be quite correct; the teacher had been visiting his fiancée; she had a red rose pinned to her dress. Croiset is particularly well known as a psychometrist, being able to describe past events with the aid of an object associated with the event he is asked to describe. An example of the astonishing accuracy he can achieve is described on page 28. However, Croiset can also give clairvoyant readings at extreme long range, often without the aid of associated objects to focus his mind. In several well-known cases, he has been able to assist the police in solving crimes. He was once able to provide American police with a sketch map which led to the finding of two murdered girls buried on a beach in North Carolina, thousands of miles away. One interesting point about some of Croiset's clairvoyant discoveries of the bodies of murder or accident victims, is that the picture he describes is sometimes that which would have been the last sight seen by the dead person, viewed actually through that person's eyes.

▼ The German parapsychologist Hans Bender (right) is one of the eminent researchers who have studied Croiset (left).

When he is asked to locate a missing person, he seems to be already aware whether or not the person is still alive.
He now operates a faith healing surgery, where he heals the sick by laying-on of hands, and has made psychic diagnoses of many illnesses which have later been confirmed only after detailed medical laboratory testing.

Padre Pio, 1887-1968, was a Capuchin monk who had some of the best-attested examples of stigmata (wounds resembling those of Christ which appear spontaneously on the body).

Like other stigmatics, Padre Pio was extremely devout and ascetic. His wounds appeared in 1918, after three years of pain and discomfort, and for the rest of his life, they exuded blood almost continuously. Padre Pio made many predictions which were subsequently confirmed, and has been associated with a number of miracles, including at least two people whose eyes were congenitally shrivelled and destroyed, and who apparently regained their sight after visiting him. Such is the following in Italy of Padre Pio that he may ultimately be canonized.

Konstantin Raudive is a Latvian expatriate who has developed an original method for communicating with spirits which appears to be less prone to interference by the subconscious mind than most other techniques of mediumship. His apparatus is simple, consisting of a tape recorder and a blank tape. The apparatus is set running, then Raudive invites the spirits to 'speak'. When the tape is played back, in between the experimenter's questions, and over the faint background hiss of the tape, can be heard voices, or snatches of speech, which may be in several different languages. Using the Raudive technique, other people have obtained the same effects, and scientifically controlled experiments have shown that the voices still appear when the medium has not handled the tape in any way, and when the tape recorder is enclosed in a Faraday cage which should blanket out any outside radiation capable of affecting the tape. Some people insist that the voices, which are not too clear, are present only in the imagination of the listener. This seems doubtful, as they have been heard by many people. They have also been ascribed to PK processes in the mind of the medium affecting the magnetic particles in the recording tape, although this would be an extremely complex application of PK.

▶ In 1935 the young Indian Kuda Bux performed the fire walk for a team of scientists.

Kuda Bux is probably the most-studied fire walker the world has seen. Fire walking was assumed to depend on trickery, until in 1935 Kuda Bux walked along a 3-metre trench filled with embers at a temperature of 430°C, without any injury. A spectator who tried to emulate the feat was badly burned, but later, several people managed to fire walk without injury.

Arnall Bloxham is an experienced hypnotist who has specialized in persuading people in a trance state to remember details of previous existences. As they recount their 'experiences', these are recorded on a tape recorder, and by now, many hundreds of hours of statements have been recorded in this way. His tapes have been examined by professional historians, who found that the information they contain was historically impeccable, and sometimes so obscure that very few people could be expected to know it. Thus it appears unlikely that the information in the tapes came from the subconscious minds of the trance subjects, or telepathically from Bloxham himself, although neither hypothesis can be completely ruled out.

Edgar Cayce, 1877-1945, was an American psychic widely known as 'The Sleeping Prophet'. He was able to prophesy only while in a state of self-induced trance. Some of his prophecies concerned the distant future, but his most notable work was in diagnosing illness and healing the sick while in a trance state. He left records of no less than 30,000 patients treated over a period of 43 years, and must be the most successful spiritual healer ever recorded. Some of his occult theories are difficult to take seriously, such as those involving Atlantis, and the significance of the pyramids, but there is no doubt that he did heal a great number of sick people very successfully, and the Cayce Foundation of America still continues to honour his life and work.

Associations etc.

Robert Leftwich is a British psychic who has gained a particular reputation as a dowser. Leftwich uses either a pair of metal rods, or the more traditional forked twig, although his 'twig' is usually made from plastic strip material. Leftwich differs from many other dowsers in that he has a strong belief in psychic powers in general, quite different from the matter-of-fact attitude taken by professional dowsers who are employed solely to find water. Leftwich has a powerful clairvoyant ability, which he puts to practical use when driving, as he believes he can vlairvoyantly 'see' around several corners ahead. He is also able to undergo out-of-the-body experiences at will, and managed to exorcize a ghost which occupied a room of his house as 'an ice-cold column.'

If you want to find out more about ESP and the paranormal, the best first step is to read up all you can on the subject. You will soon realize what a vast range of books is available, ranging from extremely serious and technical publications to some which are undoubtedly on the 'freaky' fringe. If you only read one or two source books, you will certainly obtain a very unbalanced impression of what is going on in this line of research.

Some of the more easily accessible books are listed in the bibliography on page   , but so many new ones are being published that no such listing can hope to be up-to-date.

Your next step will probably be to contact one of the various associations involved in psychic research. Once again, a warning is in order, as there are a number of groups whose activities and motivations are heavily influenced by their religious or mystical backgrounds. You should take these views into account before joining any group. Some of the smallest have resounding titles which do not necessarily reflect the value of the work they produce.

Spiritualist Association of Great Britain.
33 Belgrave Square, London SW1.
Telephone: 01-235 3351
This is an organization of spiritualist churches, whose members believe in survival after death, and in the possibility of communication with the spirits of the dead by mediums or other means. They also publish a magazine, 'Psychic researcher and Spiritualist Gazette'. Write to them for further details.

College of Psychic Studies.
16 Queensbury Place, London SW7
Telephone: 01-589 3292/3
This organization is also based on study of mediums and of spirit communication. It has a large library which is available to members (subscription £4.50 per year for associate members; full membership £6.50 per year), and also arranges sittings with approved mediums. Members receive the quarterly journal 'Light'.

Society for Psychical Research (the SPR)
1 Adam & Eve Mews, Kensington, London W8 6U9.
Telephone: 01-937 8984
The SPR is the oldest organization devoted to the study of psychic phenomena. It is still the most useful and influential organization for anyone interested in ESP and other related phenomena. Membership is £10.00 per year, and you will need a couple of references to confirm that your interest in psychic research is of a serious nature. Members receive the 'Journal' and the 'Proceedings' of the Society, free of charge, although these can be purchased by non-members. The Society holds regular meetings, and

organizes lectures from eminent researchers. It also publishes several useful booklets, such as 'Hints for sitting with mediums', and will supply a book list.

Institute of Parascience.
Sprytown, Lifton, Devon
PL1 0AY
An organization of active researchers into the paranormal. Membership includes scientists from Russia and the United States. They publish a monthly newsletter, 'Parascience'. Write for further details.

Paraphysical Laboratory
Downton, Wiltshire.
Telephone: Alderbury 361
This organization acts primarily as a clearing-house for information on research behind the Iron Curtain, and publishes the bi-monthly 'Journal of Paraphysics'. Details on application.

National Federation of Spiritual Healers.
Shortacres, Church Hill, Loughton, Essex
Telephone: 01-508 8218
The Federation can provide details of reputable healers, books, and study courses on healing. They also publish the quarterly 'Federation Review', which describes the work of spiritual healers. Details on application.

The Acupuncture Association.
2 Horroby Court, Seymour Place, London W1
Telephone: 01-723 4107
Membership is limited to qualified medical practitioners, or those who can demonstrate their expertise in acupuncture. They publish a useful register of qualified acupuncture practitioners, which may help you avoid the many charlatans practising in this field.

Harry Price Library.
University of London Library, Senate House, Malet St., London WC1
Telephone: 01-636 4514
This library contains the collection of books on the paranormal and the occult made by the late Harry Price, together with a huge range of photographs, press cuttings, and magazines, although most date from the 1930s and earlier. This is an invaluable and unique collection, and is well worth a visit.

The Radionic Association
Field House, Peaslake, Surrey GU5 9SS
Telephone: Dorking 730080
A society of qualified practitioners in medical radionics, who have passed an examination after a rigorous training course. Associate members are also admitted, and the Association publishes a journal, the 'Radionics Quarterly', and a number of booklets.

British Homoeopathic Association
27a Devonshire St, London W1N 1RJ
Telephone: 01-935 2163
This association promotes the aims and concept of homoeopathic medicine. They publish many books and leaflets, and the monthly journal 'Homoeopathy', which is available free of charge to members. Write for details and a book list.

British Society of Dowsers.
19 High St., Daventry, Northants N11 6PP
The main professional body for dowsers, which has been in existence for many years. They keep a register of competent dowsers, and publish a regular journal. Details on request.

Book list

Encyclopedia of the Unexplained
Richard Cavendish, Routledge, 1974, £7.95.
The most up-to-date reference book of its kind.

The Hidden Springs
Renée Haynes, Hutchinson, 1961, £2.75
An enquiry into the biological roots of ESP. See also her 'The seeing Eye', 1976

Parapsychology
J. B. Rhine and J. G. Pratt, Scarecrow Press, 1957, £3.60
A retrospective look by the founder of research into ESP, as we know it, and his colleague at Duke University.

The Sixth Sense
Rosalind Heywood, Chatto & Windus, 1959, £1.75
Probably the best available introduction to psychic research and its history. Dicusses in detail some of the most notable examples of ESP, including the complex 'cross-correspondence' spirit communications of the early part of this century.

The Infinite Hive
Rosalind Heywood, Pan 1966, 35p
In this sensitive book, Mrs Heywood discusses her own psychic experiences in language quite devoid of mysticism or speculation. A valuable insight into the mind of a gifted psychic.

89

The Guidebook for the Study of Psychical Research
R. H. Ashby, Rider, 1972, £2.00
An invaluable resource book for anyone interested in the paranormal. Its chief value is its detailed bibliography of standard books on the subject, graded for amateurs and advanced students. It also contains biographies of most of the eminent psychical researchers of the past, and advice on sitting with spirit mediums.

Dowsing
R. H. Leftwich, Aquarian Press, 1976
One of a comprehensive series of small books on psychic and occult powers, this book is by one of Britain's best-known dowsers, and contains much practical advice on the techniques of his art.

How to Develop Clairvoyance
W. E. Butler, Aquarian Press, 1968, 45p
Another book in the Aquarian series which contains much practical advice on clairvoyance and related abilities. It is particularly helpful in describing how to attain the special moods necessary for successful clairvoyance.

PSI: Psychic Discoveries Behind the Iron Curtain
S. Ostrander & L. Schroeder, Abacus, 1970, 95p
When it first appeared, this book caused something of a sensation, as it was the first inkling most people had of the extent of Soviet interest in the paranormal. It is an excellent survey of this otherwise inaccessible work, and contains detailed descriptions of such notable psychics as Nelya Mikhailova, and Pavlita, the inventor of 'psychotronic generators'.

The ESP Papers
S. Ostrander & L. Schroeder, Bantam, 1976, 65p
This is a useful follow-up to the previous book, and contains translations of original articles and papers first published in Russia and other Iron Curtain countries.

Supernature
L. Watson, Coronet, 50p, Hodder £3·25
Lyall Watson's book was a best-seller, breaking new ground with its attempt to find relationships between a wide range of normal and paranormal phenomena. It is a good survey of modern trends in parascience, and contains some interesting speculation.

The Romeo Error
L. Watson, Coronet, 1976, 80p
Watson speculates on the possibility of life after death in this book. If you are interested in the problem of survival and spirit communication, this is a valuable book to read, giving some unusual viewpoints which are often at variance with those usually associated with mediumship.

Dowsing: Techniques and Applications
Tom Graves, Turnstone, 1976 £3·25
A comprehensive survey of the techniques of dowsing, this is an essentially practical book, which is really a training programme for the would-be dowser. Starting with the simplest methods, the book takes you through all the common techniques, and includes a section on radiesthesia used for healing.

Superminds
John Taylor, Picador, 1976, 95p
Professor Taylor has conducted detailed studies of Uri Geller, and of other psychics who possess the power of metal-bending. This book describes his researches on Geller and others, and gives a scientist's viewpoint on their unusual powers.

Apparitions
C. Green & C. McCreery, Hamish Hamilton, 1975, £3·75
Examines apparitions from the point of view of psychic researchers. It discusses their significance and relevance to out-of-the-body experiences, hallucinations, and survival after death.

Beyond Telepathy
A. Puharich, Picador, 1975, £1·25
The states of mind necessary to produce ESP are studied in this book, and the author presents detailed theories for the workings of the paranormal. It contains descriptions of some research carried out by the author, using Faraday cages to try and define the nature of ESP. Experiments with drugs, used in an attempt to enhance ESP, are also described.

The Roots of Consciousness
J. Mishlove, Random House, 1975, £5·95
Although expensive, this book is a worthwhile addition to the library of anyone interested in the paranormal and the workings of the mind. It explores the meaning of consciousness, both in an historical context, and in the light of modern research in parapsychology. It is copiously referenced, well illustrated, and completely up-to-date.

The Link
Mathew Manning, Corgi, 1975, 75p
Mathew Manning is a young British psychic who has been associated with automatic writing, poltergeists, and a number of other phenomena. In

his autobiography, he describes how he first became aware of these paranormal abilities, and how they affected his early life.

States of Mind : ESP and Altered States of Consciousness
A. Parker, Malaby Press, 1975, £3·95
This is a rather technical, but extremely interesting book which considers all the states of mind associated with ESP. Hypnosis, drugs, dreaming, meditation, and modern techniques of biofeedback which have relevance to the study of ESP, are discussed in depth.

The Roots of Coincidence
Arthur Koestler, Picador, 1974, 60p
Physics has now gone so far beyond the boundaries which formerly defined it that it seems to break all the 'laws of nature'. Arthur Koestler argues that the new physics can be used to produce a theoretical basis for ESP. Some of the occurrences we call 'ESP' may be coincidences, brought about by a natural law which we do not yet fully understand. This has been described as one of the best short summaries of the evidence for ESP.

ESP : a scientific evaluation
C. E. M. Hansel, Macgibbon & Kee, 1966
Professor Hansel is the arch-critic of the new science of parapsychology. In this book, he could find not a single example of a paranormal event which he considered to be plausible. It is worth reading to see just how strong is the prejudice felt by some scientists against any form of research into the paranormal. Some of the alternative explanations offered may seem far less credible than the operation of ESP.

Seers, Psychics, and ESP
Milbourne Christopher, Cassell, 1970
All of the phenomena of the psychic world are described and criticized from the point of view of a stage magician, who does not believe that ESP is necessarily the explanation. Christopher gives a number of alternative explanations for common psychic events.

New Directions in Parapsychology
John Beloff (Ed.), Elek, 1974, £3·00
A survey of the current trends in parapsychology, this is a fairly technical book, but one which is well worth reading as its contents reflect the best in scientific investigation of life after death, poltergeists, animal ESP, and a number of other contemporary studies.

Galaxies of Life
S. Krippner & D. Rubin (Eds) Gordon & Breach, 1973, £2·70
Reports from an international conference of parapsychologists, covering such topics as acupuncture, Kirlian photography, and the aura. This is the only readily accessible work in these modern paths in parapsychology.

Acupuncture
Felix Mann, Pan, 1973, 50p
This is the simplest basic text on acupuncture, written by a professionally qualified practitioner, which concentrates mostly on the practical aspects, glossing over the Chinese religious basis for the art.

ESP : Beyond Time and Distance
Ghost and Divining Rod
The Monkey's Tail
Tom Lethbridge, Routledge, 1965
This series of books by Tom Lethbridge trace the development of his theories on the use of dowsing by means of the pendulum, particularly in tracing archaeological remains. They are written in an entertaining style, and contain a great deal of useful information to anyone with an interest in dowsing.

MAGAZINES AND PAPERS

In addition to the professional journals published by the various societies concerned with the paranormal, there are many other publications which you can obtain from a newsagent. Some of these are:
Psychic News
Prediction
Fate and Fortune
Spiritualist Gazette

Glossary

Agent: the sender in a telepathy experiment

Alpha feedback: a method for increasing the rate of production of alpha waves in the brain, by making them apparent to the subject.

Alpha rhythm: an electrical discharge in the brain which produces regular wave patterns when measured by an electro-encephalograph machine, attached to the scalp.

Alpha state: the condition in which the alpha rhythm is produced. It is a relaxed yet mentally alert state, which many parapsychologists believe is favourable to the production of paranormal events.

Altered state of consciousness: any condition which is not a normal waking state, such as dreaming, hypnosis, drug-induced states, and meditation. All these conditions have been associated with enhanced ESP ability.

Astral body: a psychic equivalent of the physical body, which some believe can be separated from the body under some conditions.

Astrology: a form of divination in which future events and the personality of the sitter are interpreted by reference to astronomical events.

Aura: a type of paranormal radiation which is said to surround the body, and can be seen by some psychics. Kirlian photography is sometimes said to reveal the aura.

Automatism: action which is not controlled by the conscious mind, such as automatic writing.

Biofeedback: a technique for making us aware of functions which are normally imperceptible (such as the alpha rhythm).

Call: a subject's response or guess in an ESP test.

Clairvoyance: a type of ESP in which information is gained without the use of the normal senses, and without the assistance of another person's mind (as in *Telepathy*).

Control: an apparently disembodied intelligence which directs a medium in a trance state. It may be either a spirit entity or a *secondary personality* of the medium, which is usually hidden.

Cross correspondence: a communication received by a medium which cross-refers to a message received via another person, and is thus regarded as being proof of the validity of the communication.

Depersonalization: a feeling of unreality and 'not belonging in one's own body'. A psychiatric condition, as well as a description of the state of mind in which *Out-of-the-body experiences* occur.

Decline effect: the falling-off of scores which often occurs in prolonged ESP experiments.

Divination: using psychic power to predict future events, usually with the aid of a crystal ball, tea-leaves, ouija, etc.

Dowsing: finding water, buried objects, etc., by divination.

EEG: electroencephalograph; a machine which records the electrical activity of the brain by means of electrodes attached to the scalp.

Ectoplasm: a substance said to be produced by mediums, which can assume the shape of spirits or of dead persons.

ESP Extrasensory perception: awareness of an event or of another person's state of mind without the use of the normal senses. Strictly speaking, it includes only *telepathy, clairvoyance, precognition* and *retrocognition*.

Guide: see *Control*.

Hit: an accurate response in an ESP test.

Hypnosis: a trance state in which the subject is extremely susceptible to suggestions made by the person who has induced the trance. Often induced in an attempt to enhance ESP.

I Ching: the *Book of Changes;* an ancient Chinese manual on the interpretation of thrown yarrow stalks; a highly respected and psychologically subtle form of divination.

Levitation: lifting of the entire body (or objects) by paranormal means. A few mediums have been recorded as levitating successfully.

Lucid dream: a type of dream in which the sleeper is aware that he is dreaming, and is able to influence the content of the dream. Sometimes associated with telepathic dream states.

Meditation: a form of mental state where concentration is turned inward, and consciousness seems to be expanded.

Medium: a person with the ability to enter a trance state in which the medium has access to information not otherwise available.

Mesmerism: method of inducing a hypnotic state, originally invented by Mesmer.

OOBE (or OBE) Out-of-the-body experience: a mental state in which a person finds himself located mentally outside the body, and often 'looking at himself'.

Ouija: Simple device for communicating with spirits, or receiving messages from the subconscious mind. From the

French and German words for 'yes', *oui* and *ja*.

Paranormal: an event which cannot be interpreted according to the currently accepted laws of nature.

Parapsychology: the scientific study of paranormal events associated with mental activity.

Pendulum: a small weight on a string, used in dowsing.

PK—Psychokinesis: moving objects purely with the power of the mind.

Planchette: a device holding a pencil which is used to produce automatic writing.

Poltergeist: an outbreak of paranormal phenomena in which objects are moved about or flung with no apparent source. Adolescents are often associated with poltergeists, although they are not the conscious cause. Probably a form of unwitting PK.

Possession: a state in which a person's mind appears to be taken over and controlled by another person or spirit.

Precognition: acquiring knowledge of future events by paranormal means.

PSI: an abbreviation which can refer to any aspect of the paranormal.

PSI hitting: consistently scoring better than chance would predict in an ESP test.

PSI missing: consistently missing an ESP target. Common in people sceptical of ESP, who score much lower than chance would predict; and therefore equally paranormal in nature.

Psychic: an early term for a person with paranormal ability.

Psychometry: a form of clairvoyance in which an object acts as a focus for a medium's interpretation of past events.

Radiesthesia: the use of paranormal powers for diagnosis of disease and for healing, through an intermediary device such as a pendulum or a specially designed machine.

Radionics: the basic theory of radiesthesia.

Random numbers: numbers produced by mathematical means or by a machine, which avoid any bias in the selection of targets for an ESP test.

Reincarnation: doctrine which supposes that the personality survives death and can be reborn in another individual. An important part of several major religions.

Retrocognition: knowledge of past events by paranormal means.

Seance: a session at which a medium uses paranormal abilities to convey information to others present.

Secondary personality: an altered state of consciousness in which it appears that a different mind is present in a person. In *multiple personality*, several minds seem to appear at different times. Sometimes an indication of mental illness.

Sheep and goats: terms coined to describe those who believe in the paranormal and who generally score at above chance levels in ESP tests (sheep), while the sceptic goat scores at below levels predicted by chance.

Sitters: persons consulting a medium or attending a seance.

Spiritualism: a religion which communicates with the spirits of the dead, via mediums, and also promotes healing by psychic means.

Subject: a person being studied for some psychic ability.

Target: an object, picture, or word which is the subject in an ESP test is trying to identify.

Tarot cards: deck of cards often used for divination, bearing extremely ancient symbolic designs.

Telepathy: direct communication between two minds by means of ESP.

Trance: an altered state of consciousness in which information in the subconscious mind can come to the surface. Alternatively, the mind may be open to communication with spirits.

Translocation (or **teleportation**): poorly documented paranormal power in which an object is instantaneously moved from one point to another, and may pass through solid objects without leaving any trace. Appears to contravene all the known laws of physics.

Travelling clairvoyance: similar to out-of-the-body experiences, in which a person reports having been mentally transported to a distance, and having observed events there.

Zener cards: cards used as targets in tests of telepathy and clairvoyance. They bear simple geometric symbols; circle, cross, square, star, wavy lines.

Index

Numbers in italics indicate illustrations.

Aberfan disaster, 38-9, *39*
Acupuncture, 64-6, *64*, *65*
Acupuncture Association, The 89
Agent, 92
Alexandra, Empress of Russia, 85
Alexis, Czarevitch, 85
Alpha feedback, 92
Alpha rhythm, 14, 23, 92
Alpha state, 92
Altered state of consciousness, 14, 79, 92
Animal ESP, 54-6, *54-5*, *56*
Animal magnetism, 10, 84
Animal navigation, 57, *57*
Animal precognition, 54-5, *57*
Animals: 'educated', 54; faith healing of, 68; homing behaviour of, 57; sacrifice of, 9; 'sixth sense of, 7, 54
Arigo (Brazilian healer), 67
Astral body, *34*, 92
Astral travel, 35-6
Astrology, *10*, 37, 92
Aura, 60, 92
Automated equipment (for ESP trials), *16-17*
Automatic dice rolling machine, *18*
Automatic drawings, *44*, 45
Automatic music composition, *26*
Automatic paintings, *30*
Automatic writing, 27-8, 29-30, *30*, 44-5, *44*, 78, 79
Automatism, 92

Bach, Dr, 66
Backster, Cleve, 61-2
Beeton, Mrs, 45
Biofeedback, 22-3, *23*, 92
Bishop's Rule (dowsing), 72
Bladud (druid), 84
Bloxham, Arnall, 32-3, *33*, 87
Box, Kudha, *87*
Brazil, 26, 27

British Homoeopathic Association, 89
British Society of Dowsers, 89
Broad, Professor, 30
Brown, Rosemary, *26*

Call, 92
Cathars, *31*
Cats, homing ability of, 57
Cayce, Edgar, 87
Cayce Foundation of America, 87
Cheops, the Great Pyramids of, 82
Clairvoyance, 4, 9-10, 11, 12-17, *15*, 28, 36, 74-5, 86, 92
Cloud chamber, 69
College of Psychic Studies, 88-9
Controls (spirit guides), 28-30, *30*, 92
Cook, Florence (medium), 85
Croiset, Gerard, *28-9*, 86
Crookes, Sir William, 85
Cross Correspondences, 29-30, 92
Crowley, Aleister, *8*
Crystal ball, *37*, 79

Davenport, Ira and William, 84
Dean, Douglas, 58
Decline effect, 92
Dee, John, 9-10, *10*
Depersonalization, 35, 92
Devil, 9, *11*
Dice-throwing, *18*, 19, 77
Disasters, premonition of, 37-40, *38*, *39*
Divination, 37, *37*, 79, 92
Dixon, Jeanne, 40
Dogs, homing ability of, 57
Dowsing, 6, 70-3, *71*, *73*, 88, 92; from afar, 73; pendulum, 71-2; rods, 71, 88; techniques, 72-3; twig, 71, 88
Drawings: automatic, *44*, 45; reproduction by Geller of, 45-6, *46*
Drbal, Karle, 82
Dreams, 50-3, *50-1*, *52*, *53*; experiments, 51-2; lucid, 92; prophetic, 37-8, 50-1; transmitting, 53
Dürer, Albrecht, *44*, 45

Ectoplasm, 47-8, *47*, 92
Egyptian soul or *bah*, 36

Elawar, Imad, 32
Electroencephalograph (EEG), 13, 14, 36, 45, 58, 92
'Elizabeth', 24
Elizabeth I, Queen, automatic drawing of, 44
Emotional plants, 60-2
Enochian language, 10
ESP trials, 16, *16-17*
Estebany, 68-9
Euclid, 9
Evans, Colin, *19*
Eysenck, Prof. Hans, 14

F. & D. A. (USA), 69
Faith healing, 67-9, *68*
Faraday Cage, *14*, 16, 87
Firewalkers, *25*
Flash photography, 48
Floating object, PK ability to move, 77
Flower essence healing, 66
Fortune telling, *37*
Fox sisters (Margaret and Kate), 10-11, 42, 84
Franklin, Benjamin, 10
Franklin, Sir John, *28*
Fringe medicine, 64-9

Geller, Uri, 18, 45-6, *45*, *46*, 59
German ESP test machine, *16-17*
Guirdham, Arthur, *31*
Guthrie, Malcolm, *15*

Hallucinations, 35
Harry Price Library, 89
Hemingway, Ernest, 34
Hit, 92
Home, Daniel Dunglas, 42-3, *42*, 85
Homoeopathy, 66
Houdini, Harry, 80, 85-6
Hunting the thimble, 82
Hurkos, Peter *15*
Hypnotism, hypnosis, 10, 11, 23, 32, *33*, 53, *68*, 79, 84, 87, 92; stigmata and, 24-5

I Ching, 92
Indian Rope Trick, 10, 22, *80*
Ink Blot test, *37*
Institute of Parascience, 89

Kamensky, 58
Kelly, Edward, 9-10
Kennedy, President John F,

39, 40
Kennedy, Robert, 40
King, Martin Luther, 40, 53
Kirlian, Semyon, 59
Kirlian photography, *44*, 59-60, *60-1*, 65, 69, 92
Koestler, Arthur, 34
Kotsoudis, Rodinos, *23*

Lang, Fritz, 62
Lateau, Louise, 24
Lawrence, D. H., 34
Lechler, Dr, 24
Leftwich, Robert, 88
'Leopold' (control), *30*
Lethbridge, Tom, 73
Levitation, 11, *11*, *18*, *19*, 20, 42-3, *42*, 48, *48-9*, 49, 84, 92
Lie detectors, 61
Life after death, *5*, 11, 26-30, *27*, 34, 78
Loach, Ethel de, 59

Magic pyramid, 82-3, *83*
'Magic' tricks, 80-3, *80*, *81*, *82*, *83*
Magicians, 9, *9*, 10, *10*, 46, 81
Magnetic passes, 10
Maimonides Dream Laboratory, New York, 52
Manning, Mathew, 43-5, *44*
Meditation, 92
Mediums, 9, 11, 14, *18*, *24-5*, 26-30, *26*, *27*, *30*, *37*, 42-5, *42*, 78-9, *79*, 84, 85, 92; fraudulent, 47-9, *47*, *48-9*, 79, 80
Mesmer, Friedrich, 10, 84
Mesmerism, 92
Mesopotamia, 9
Metal-bending, 45, *45*
Mikhailova, Nelya (Nelya Kulagina), 20, *21*, 58
Mind-reading trick, 82
Miracles, 67-8
Mitchell, Ed., 16
Multiple personality, 93
Murphy, Bridey, *31*
Myers, F. W. H., 29-30
Mystics, 22-3; stigmata produced by, 23-4

National Federation of Spiritual Healers, 89
Neumann, Teresa, *22*
Nicolaiev, 58

Occult, the, 9-11, *8*, *9*, *27*, *34*
Ouija board, 27, 79, 92
Oliver, Isaac (spirit), *44*
Orgone accumulator, 69
'Out of the body' experiences (OOBE's), 34-6, *34*, *35*, *36*, 92

Pain, control of, 23
Palladino, Eusapia, 48-9, 85
Parascience, 58-63; the machines of, 62-3
Paranormal, the (PSI), *4-5*, 6, 92; science and, 6-7, *6*
Paraphysical Laboratory, 89
Parapsychology, 10, *17*, 25, 63, 92
Pavlità, Robert, 60
Pavlita Generators, 60
Pendulums: dowsing, 71-2, 93; PK ability to move, 76-7; talking, 80-1, *81*
Philippines: psychic surgeons in, 67, *67*
Photography: Kirlian, *44*, 59-60, *60-1*; psychic, 58-60, *59*
Pio, Padre, 86-7
Planchette, 27-8, 78, 93
Plants: emotional, 60-2; faith healing, 69
Poltergeists, 20, *20*, 43, 76, 84, 93
Polygraph machines, 61
Possession, 93
Pratt, Dr, 15
Precognition, 63, 93; animal, 54-5, *57*
Premonitions, 37-40, *38*, *39*, *41*
Priest-magicians, *9*
Prophecy, *9*, *10*, 37, 84, 87
Prophetic dreams, 37-8, 50-1, 52
PSI, 93
PSI hitting, 93
PSI-trailing, 57
Psychic bonds, 13-14
Psychic frauds, 47-9, *47*, *48-9*, 80-3, *80*, *81*, *82*, *83*, 84, 85
'Psychic' photography, 58-60, *59*, *60-1*
Psychic surgery, 66-7, *67*
Psychokinesis (PK), 4, 6, 18-20, *18*, *19*, *20*, *21*, 25, 55-6, 60, 62, 63, *63*, 76-7, 81, 87, 93
Psychometrist, *28*, 86
Psychosomatic disorders, 64
Psychotronic generators, 60

R101 airship, premonitions about crash of, 38, *38*
Radiesthesia, 69, *69*, 93
Radio-active random number generators, 55, 63
Radionic Association, The, 89
Radionics, 93
Raising the dead, *10*
Randi, 46
Random numbers, 55, 63, 93
Rapid Eye Movement (REM) sleep, 51
Rasputin, Grigori, 85
Raudive, Konstantin, 87
Recording scores, 74-5
Reich, Wilhelm, 69
Reincarnation, 31-3, *31*, *32-3*, 93
Relaxation techniques, 23
Retrocognition, 93
Rhine, J. B., *6*, 14-16, 19, 58, 75
Robertson, Morgan, 39
Russell, Bertrand, 45
Russia, psychic research in, 20, *21*, 58, 60, 62

Sauvin, Paul, 62
Schmidt, Helmut, 19
Schmidt PK testing machines, 19, *62*, 63, *63*
Scrying, 9, 79
Seances, 11, *11*, *18*, 26-7, 27, 42-3, 47-9, *47*, *48-9*, 78-9, *79*, 93
Secondary personality, 93
Serios, Ted, *43*, 58
Shamans (priest magicians), 9
Shelley, Mark, *46*
Shipton, Mother, 84
Singapore religious parade, *24-5*
Smith, Mlle, *30*
Smoke, PK ability to move, 76
Society for Psychical Research (SPR), 11, 26, 30, 48, 74, 88
Spirit guides ('controls'), 28-30, *30*
Spirit (phantom) hands, 42-3, *42*, 48, 84
Spirit rappings, 10-11, 42, 48, *48*, 49, 84
Spiritism (Brazil), 26
Spiritualism, 10-11, 26-7, *27*, 93
Spiritualist Association of Great Britain, 88
Spiritualist surgeons, *67*
Spoon-bending, 18, 45, *46*

95

Stevenson, Ian, 32
Stigmata, *22*, 23-4, 86-7;
  hypnotism and, 24-5, *24*-5
Survival after death, *5*, 11,
  26-30, *27*, 34

Table rapping/tipping, 27, *48*
'Talking' horses, 54
Talking pendulums, 80-1, *81*
Tape recorder, spirit
  communication with, 87
Tarot cards, *8*, 93
Tart, Charles, 36
Tea leaves, reading of, *37*
Telepathic morse, 58, 62

Telepathy, 4, 12-17, *12*, *13*, *14*,
  15, 25, 27, 28, 58, *58*, 74-5, 93
Thoughtographs, *43*, 59
Titanic, premonitions about
  sinking of, 38, *38*, 39-40, *41*
Transcendental meditation, 14
Trances, 26, *27*, *30*, 47, *47*,
  84, 87, 93
Translocation, 93
Transpersonal consciousness,
  36
Travelling clairvoyance, 93
Twain, Mark, 50-1
Twins, close affinity of, 12-13

Vietnam, 70
Voodoo death, 74

Watts, Mrs Alaric, *30*
Witchcraft, 9, *11*
Woodruff, 15, 16
Woolf, Virginia, 34
Worrall, Olga, 69
The Wreck of the Titan, 39-40

Yogis, 14

Zen, 14
Zener cards, 14-16, 49, 52, 53,
  74-5, 93

Credits

Artists
Tim Earnshaw
Ron Hayward Art Group
QED
Graham Rogers
John Shackell

Photographs
Aldus Books: 10, 61, 79, 88
Anglia Press Agency: 55
Barnaby's Picture Library: 24, 25
Nick Birch: 27

John H. Cutten: 15, 18, 30,
  42, 47, 60, 61, 67, 84, 85
Michael Holford: 8, 36
Eric Hosking F.R.P.S.: 54-55
Leifgeiges: 17, 53, 86
The Mansell Collection: 11
Marshall Cavendish: Contents
  6, 43, 66, 71
Philips Records: 26
Popperfoto: 31, 39, 85
Harry Price Library:
  Contents, 22, 78, 84, 85, 87
Psychic News: 18, 19, 20
Radio Times Hulton Picture
  Library: 9, 23, 37, 38, 40
  84, 85

Snark International: 36
Neville Spearman: 31
Syndication International:
  Contents, 45, 46
Tate Gallery: 32
John Topham Picture Library:
  69, 79, 86
John Watney: 35
Van Duren Contract
  Publications Ltd: 44
Western Mail & Echo: 33
Zefa: 64, 65

Cover
Design: Design Machine
Photograph: Alex Von Koettlitz